MYSTERIES
OF THE
ANCIENT WORLD

Prepared by the Special Publications Division
National Geographic Society, Washington, D. C.

MYSTERIES OF THE ANCIENT WORLD

Contributing Authors: CHRISTINE K. ECKSTROM, RON FISHER, LOUIS DE LA HABA, TEE LOFTIN, TOM MELHAM, H. ROBERT MORRISON, CYNTHIA RUSS RAMSAY, JUDITH E. RINARD, GENE S. STUART, GEORGE E. STUART

Contributing Photographers: NATHAN BENN, JAMES P. BLAIR, ROBERT FRESON, GORDON W. GAHAN, FRED MAROON, JEAN VERTUT, ADAM WOOLFITT

Paintings by ROY ANDERSON

Published by THE NATIONAL GEOGRAPHIC SOCIETY
ROBERT E. DOYLE, *President*
MELVIN M. PAYNE, *Chairman of the Board*
GILBERT M. GROSVENOR, *Editor*
MELVILLE BELL GROSVENOR, *Editor Emeritus*

Prepared by THE SPECIAL PUBLICATIONS DIVISION
ROBERT L. BREEDEN, *Editor*
DONALD J. CRUMP, *Associate Editor*
PHILIP B. SILCOTT, *Senior Editor*
MERRILL WINDSOR, *Consulting Editor*
WILLIAM R. GRAY, *Managing Editor*
SALLIE M. GREENWOOD, PATRICIA F. FRAKES, SUDHA IRWIN, KAREN M. KOSTYAL, LUIS TORRES, *Researchers*

Illustrations and Design
DON A. SPARKS, *Picture Editor*
URSULA PERRIN VOSSELER, *Art Director*
CHRISTINE K. ECKSTROM, TONI EUGENE, RON FISHER, LOUIS DE LA HABA, TEE LOFTIN, TOM MELHAM, H. ROBERT MORRISON, CYNTHIA RUSS RAMSAY, JUDITH E. RINARD, GENE S. STUART, SUZANNE VENINO, *Picture Legends*
JOHN D. GARST, JR., CHARLES W. BERRY, MARGARET DEANE GRAY, DEWEY G. HICKS, JR., CATHY WELLS, *Map Research, Design, and Production*

Production and Printing
ROBERT W. MESSER, *Production Manager*
GEORGE V. WHITE, *Assistant Production Manager*
RAJA D. MURSHED, JUNE L. GRAHAM, CHRISTINE A. ROBERTS, DAVID V. SHOWERS, *Production Assistants*
DEBRA A. ANTONINI, BARBARA BRICKS, JANE H. BUXTON, ROSAMUND GARNER, TURNER HOUSTON, SUZANNE J. JACOBSON, MARIANNE R. KOSZORUS, BETH MOLLOY, CLEO PETROFF, KATHERYN M. SLOCUM, SUZANNE VENINO, ALISON WILBUR, *Staff Assistants*
GEORGE I. BURNESTON, III, *Index*

Second Printing 1985

Overleaf: Massive stone statues, their significance shrouded by time, gaze eternally upon the hills of Easter Island. Page 1: Towering 450 feet in the glow of a setting sun, the Great Pyramid at Giza symbolizes the mysterious legacies of the ancient world. Hardcover design: Engraved on a gold ring, Mycenaean hunters chase game in a chariot.

CONTENTS

Steatite seals, intricately incised with strange animals and enigmatic script, evoke the Harappan civilization of ancient India, which flourished more than 4,000 years ago and then faded away.

NATIONAL GEOGRAPHIC PHOTOGRAPHER JAMES P. BLAIR, NATIONAL MUSEUM OF PAKISTAN, KARACHI

PHOTO RESEARCHERS, INC.; HARDCOVER DESIGN: EKDOTIKE ATHENON S.A., NATIONAL ARCHAEOLOGICAL MUSEUM, ATHENS

INTRODUCTION:
ENIGMAS
FROM THE PAST

by GEORGE E. STUART

*Archeologist, National
Geographic Society*

NATIONAL GEOGRAPHIC PHOTOGRAPHER
VICTOR R. BOSWELL, JR., ANTHROPOS
MORAVSKÉ MUZEUM, BRNO

NATHAN BENN, MUSEUM OF
ANATOLIAN CIVILIZATIONS, ANKARA

Evidence of the past lies all around us. A grandparent's favorite rocking chair, for instance, is a familiar reminder of days gone by. Other reminders, however, are strange and perplexing, for they reach out to us from mysterious peoples and from ancient times—the towering pyramids of Egypt, the vibrant frescoes from the ruins of Minoan Crete, the giant stone figures of Easter Island.

Such legacies, scattered throughout the world, afford us haunting traces of the cultures and civilizations that are part of our distant past. These traces have cast a spell upon us all. Intrigued, we puzzle over who created these wondrous things, and why.

I recall standing as a boy of 12 before an Indian mound that lay in a shadowy river swamp near my hometown of Camden, South Carolina. Overcome by a sense of awe and intense curiosity, I couldn't help but wonder: Who had built the mound, and when? Where had they come from and where gone? Were they as uneasy in that forbidding place as I was?

That incident helped me decide to become an archeologist, a scientist who is trained to recognize and to interpret clues from the rubble of the human past. By studying remains ranging from flecks of charred food in a long-dead campfire to spectacular treasures of gold from royal tombs, we slowly begin to understand and to appreciate the peoples of yesterday.

Often the results are startling.

North America's European settlers, for example, simply could not believe that the thousands of flat-topped mounds and contoured earthworks in the forests east of the Mississippi River were the works of "savage" Indians. Wild speculation attributed these edifices to a lost race of giants, to wandering Egyptians or Phoenicians, or to refugees from sunken Atlantis.

During the past century, scholars have put together the general sweep of the real story: The builders of the mounds were neither mythical beings nor Old World wanderers. They were the ancestors of the Creeks, the Cherokees, and other tribes the European settlers met—the Southeastern Indians who raised imposing temples, created complex religious art, populated thriving towns, and established vast trade networks that extended from the Gulf of Mexico to the Great Lakes.

Fanciful theories also grew up around a large wheel-shaped stone pattern near the top of a peak in Wyoming. Known as the Bighorn Medicine Wheel, the structure is 80 feet across and has 28 "spokes." The mystifying design was said by some to be the work of Aztecs, of Hindus, of Chinese, or of the ubiquitous seafaring Phoenicians. After on-site study in the early 1970's, astronomer

Artwork from long ago reveals the diversity and sophistication of ancient peoples. Clockwise from top: a reconstructed necklace of shells and fox teeth from Ice Age Europe; a stone plaque of an embracing couple and a mother and child excavated from Çatal Hüyük in Turkey; an ivory figurine of the Egyptian ruler Cheops; a mask of molded terracotta unearthed in the Indus Valley; a chiseled stone ball discovered on the Orkney Islands off Scotland; a frog-shaped gold bead from Minoan Crete; an embossed gold cup found in a Mycenaean tomb in Greece; a terracotta bust of an Etruscan warrior of ancient Italy; a tapa-cloth figure from Easter Island.

John A. Eddy suggested that this "wheel" was built as a
rudimentary astronomical observatory, with which early Indians
of the Great Plains identified the day of the summer solstice. By
so doing, they had the basis for a calendar and could set dates
for their ceremonies.

In Rhodesia, in much the same way, the masonry walls and
conical tower of Great Zimbabwe fired the imagination. The
impressive ruins were variously thought to be an Arab or Asian
outpost, or the Biblical Ophir—the source of King Solomon's gold.
But the efforts of two generations of archeologists have dispelled the
myths. Zimbabwe was, in fact, a religious and trading center of the
rich and powerful Shona peoples in the centuries after A.D. 1400.

In recent years, a curious theory has emerged that such great
accomplishments of the human past owe their inspiration to beings
from other worlds. Not only is this an unwarranted slur on human
intelligence, but it also disregards the evidence at hand, which
shows the ancient world to have been a place of complexity
and accomplishment.

The anonymous artists who painted cave walls in France and
Spain 16,000 years ago did not differ physically or mentally from
people in the world today. They possessed the same intellectual
capacity and the same creative ability, which they adapted
perfectly to their own time and place. They probably puzzled over
the same kinds of human problems as you and I, and doubtless they
had hopes and aspirations comparable to our own. Likewise, the
creators of Stonehenge and other megaliths of western Europe were
capable of understanding the mathematics involved in establishing
these astronomical observatories. As archeologist Colin Renfrew
noted, "The greatest mystery of the megaliths is that so many
people have felt compelled to attribute them to outsiders, rather than
acknowledging the ageless, universal power of human ingenuity
and imagination."

In the chapters of this book, we explore nine great episodes in
the long and fascinating human epic. This handful, of course, is only
representative; many more could be chosen from all corners of the
globe and from all ages of mankind.

Because the artifacts survive from as long ago as twelve million
yesterdays, our retrospective view is often veiled in mystery. Many
of the episodes provoke questions that have no simple or obvious
answers. We can only follow the progress of anthropologists,
archeologists, ethnologists, art historians, linguists, astronomers,
and other scholars as they seek to fashion the mosaic of the past from
scattered fragments and to reaffirm the power of the human mind.

IN HIDDEN CAVES

by GENE S. STUART

photographed by JEAN VERTUT
and ROBERT FRESON

The first flakes of a February snowstorm brushed silently against the windows of the small three-car electric train I rode through the winding river valleys of southwestern France. The somber light of that winter afternoon darkened perceptibly as we entered a gorge of steep gray cliffs. Moments later, the train rounded a bend and began to slow as we neared Les Eyzies. This tiny village harbors several ancient rock-shelters that have been used intermittently for more than 30,000 years. Here, in the deep of winter, I would begin to search for my oldest modern ancestors, Cro-Magnon hunters who lived in Europe during the last stages of the Ice Age, 10,000 to 37,000 years ago.

I have long been fascinated by these hardy people, whose harsh existence I have never envied, but who left an inspiring legacy of art and handiwork. At best I hoped to gain an appreciation of their difficult way of life. I dared not expect many insights into the unsolved mysteries that surround the earliest works of art in the world—paintings and carvings created by unknown artists shrouded in forgotten cycles of time. Who had made these masterpieces? What was their significance? And why had the people ventured into dark, haunting caves to produce them?

As I stepped off the train, I felt a penetrating chill; but theirs, I knew, had been a time of truly bitter cold. Although fluctuations in climate periodically warmed the earth, gleaming glaciers at times covered the land. Snow lay in sheltered coves until late June, and silent starry nights often transformed heavy dew into crystals of frost. By November new blankets of snow lay across the land. January's howling winds and swirling storms drove herds of game—reindeer, horses, bison—to protected valleys where they gathered for warmth. Muscular, fur-clad men watched the movements of the herds and stealthily hunted them.

During the coldest period, all of Scandinavia and most of Germany and Poland were locked beneath a vast ice sheet. Ice covered most of Ireland and all of Scotland; southern England was ice-free and habitable. Europe's shoreline spread farther than it does today. England joined France; Italy and Sicily formed a single peninsula. The region south of the ice sheet, from southern England into Russia, was the belt of habitation, the life-support zone for animals and the hunters who pursued them—the first modern people of Europe.

The paintings left by these people were discovered in caves in France and Spain within the last century. One of these, Les Combarelles, yawns in a recess in a cliff east of Les Eyzies. On an icy morning I followed custodian Claude Archambeau into the darkness and, seemingly, back thousands of years in time. In the narrow, dimly lit corridor his shape loomed before me in silhouette, appearing almost like an ancient artist on his way to a secret task. A friend of mine, local innkeeper André Bousquet, walked close beside me, his gray hair protected by a felt hat against cold water dripping from the cavern ceiling.

As we walked, Claude pointed out lines scratched into the stone walls. Finally he stopped and took my arm. "Look," he whispered. I peered at the wall, and suddenly an eerie image swirled into focus— a lioness in profile. She held her head with dignity. Her eye was alert,

Overleaf: Cracked with age, clay bison sculpted some 16,000 years ago survive in the secluded blackness of France's Le Tuc d'Audoubert cave. Their presence mystifies scholars seeking clues to the people who created the world's first known art during the harsh period toward the end of the Ice Age.

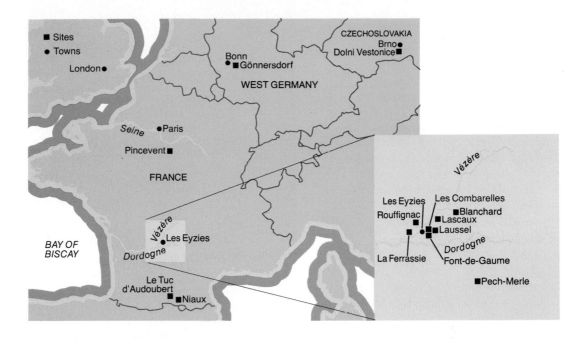

her chin defiant. But spears had been thrust upward into her side, and pale foam cascaded from her mouth and onto the rocks below. I stood transfixed by the beauty of this image, amazed that it had been incised with a sharp flint tool probably 13,000 years ago. Claude spoke softly of the artists who had carved these walls and of the precision of their handiwork. As he talked, his fingers flicked near the aged lines as if he, too, held a razor-sharp flint tool. Already I had found a link to my ancestors.

Elsewhere in the cave, I saw engravings of familiar beings: men and women, a horse with a smug smile, a pacing bear, a tiny fawn. I followed the men through narrow twisting passageways, losing all sense of time and direction. Distances meant nothing. Day became night in the underside of the earth's surface as I followed the muted footfalls and flickering lights, which at times seemed like the torches of prehistory.

When we returned to the cave mouth, fat snowflakes obliterated the shapes of trees and cliffs around us. The cold brought tears that stung my cheeks. I breathed, and a shaft of wind bit the back of my throat. I had seen some of the ancients' treasures, and now, I reflected, I sensed a part of their frigid world.

André and I slowly drove the short distance back to Les Eyzies through the deepening snow, following a swift stream called the Vézère. The village is sheltered by cliffs, and the snow there was less deep, the wind not so piercing.

I thought of the reindeer, ibex, red deer, bison, pigs, horses, and cattle of ancient times that had found shelter there, and of those animals that had fallen prey to the hunters who awaited them. These people made winter camps in cave entrances and in rock-shelters. Wearing robes and other clothing of skin and fur, using hide tents and windbreaks, and building fires to warm *(Continued on page 18)*

In nomadic hunting camps and temporary settlements, bands of Ice Age hunters lived scattered across a region that stretched from southern England east into Russia. During thousands of years of the Upper Paleolithic, or late Old Stone Age, vast ice sheets advanced and retreated, bringing a fluctuating and unstable climate to these first modern people of Europe.

uted colors of early autumn—a foreshadowing of cold weather—speckle trees in the Vézère valley near the village of Les Eyzies, France. During the winters of the Ice Age, herds of reindeer, horses, bison, and other game gathered in this sheltered valley. People followed the animals here to hunt them. At times, they entered the many nearby caves and decorated the walls with art. An eerie glow beyond custodian Claude Archambeau (below) marks the natural entrance to one of these caves, Les Combarelles. Steps and a paved floor give access to present-day visitors.

With stealth and skill, hunters of 30,000 years ago set an ambush for a band of reindeer grazing in the Vézère valley. A successful

kill will yield meat, skins for tents and clothing, and bones and antlers for tools—all necessary for survival. Such Ice Age people wintered in small groups in rock-shelters along overhanging cliffs. Spring thaw lured the animals to other ranges, and the hunters probably followed.

Imposing images of aurochs, horses, and deer (right) surge across the ceiling of the French cave of Lascaux. Such paintings may have expressed religious thoughts, given life to mythological tales, re-created important events, or symbolized game the artists hoped to kill. A painter of ancient times (below) blows powdered pigment through a tube to leave an outlined handprint—possibly his signature or simply a mark of his passing. Such handprints frame a pair of horses in the cave of Pech-Merle in France. Jacques Marsal (below, right), guide and overseer at Lascaux, found the cave with a group of friends while exploring surrounding woods in 1940. The very discovery of such caves, however, often threatens them by attracting people and thus altering the environment within.

the shelters, I imagine that they must have found relative comfort.

"The hunters near Les Eyzies killed mostly reindeer," Arthur Spiess had told me. Tall and scholarly, Art, now an archeologist with the Maine Historic Preservation Commission, has spent several months studying the habits of the hunters. "We know much about their diet from excavating their winter camps. They knew the ways of the herds of game as well as any modern rancher knows his cattle." Though game was not always plentiful, extra meat could have been stored in the frozen ground or in an icy bog. And a hunter wrapped in warm lynx fur, relaxing beside a glowing fire while dining on unborn fawn, could not have felt that his life was always such a difficult one.

Although archeologists know something of the winter habits of the hunters, their whereabouts and livelihood in spring and summer remain mysteries. They probably did not move far away—only far enough to follow the herds to other ranges and to gather wild plants.

Archeologist Martin Wobst of the University of Massachusetts believes that they lived in bands of about 25 people. "Each band probably traveled within its own territory," he had told me. "And I'm sure they made contact from time to time with other bands."

"Yet we don't know what social organization they had," added Art Spiess. "We can't even say for certain that they lived in family groups. It's possible they were organized into systems we haven't even thought of."

The bands they lived in were scattered. The population was sparse. I was amazed when Martin told me, "In all of present-day southern England there were probably no more than 500 people." In 1960 Edward S. Deevey, Jr., a biologist then with Yale University, estimated that the population of the entire world around 25,000 years ago was only some 3.34 million, about the number of people living in Chicago today.

They were strong and husky, these ancient hunters—long-legged, muscular, and with a mental capacity as great as or greater than our own. Some experts think the birthrate was moderately high—but the mortality rate was higher. Half the population died by the age of 15. Females lived only into their late 20's, on the average, and males into their early 30's. Those who lived longer were probably respected as wise advisers. Well-preserved skeletons not only help us visualize the people but also, having been carefully buried, show us their belief in an afterlife. Art Spiess explained what can be learned from the burial customs. "Graves occasionally contain stone tools," he said. "Animal bones near the skeletons indicate that people may have been buried with chunks of meat. Nobody provides the dead with useful things like those unless there is a belief that they will be needed in the future."

The ancients also were buried in finery. Bracelets of bone circle skeletal arms. Thousands of ivory, shell, or bone beads lie where they once adorned skin clothing. Buttons and long pins held tunics or cloaks in place. Northeast of Moscow, archeologists found the graves of two young boys, laid head to head. Their funerary attire included a cap, trousers, tunics, and moccasinlike shoes. Ice Age art portrays men with beards and mustaches and women with elaborately parted or braided hair.

18

Yet, knowing all this, I still could not grasp what an individual had looked like until I traveled to Paris and visited the Musée de l'Homme—the Museum of Man. With Pierre Becquelin, a dark-eyed, dark-haired archeologist on the museum staff, I walked among exhibits showing the development of mankind. We saw the evolution of stone tools from crude choppers to finely chipped flint knives, and the physical development of humans from early primates to modern people. Finally, we paused before the skull of an Ice Age woman who had died at about the age of 20. Her face had been slender, her forehead high and rounded. Pierre listened as I tried to re-create what she might have looked like. Partway through my description, I felt a sudden jolt of surprise. The woman I was portraying could have been me. "You have made a great discovery," Pierre said with a smile. "Anyone who studies these people for any length of time quickly finds how much like us they were in size, looks, and intellect."

Later that day, I walked beside the Seine, my woolen cap pulled low against the windblown snow, and I thought of the Ice Age summer encampment of Pincevent that once stood on the riverbank 45 miles to the southeast. There, hunters had lain in wait for reindeer crossing at a shallow ford. Their campfires and butchering tools gradually had been covered by layers of mud and silt, only to be unearthed thousands of years later by archeologists. I glanced at the Seine, flowing swiftly and flooding the quays where normally lovers stroll and old men nod over fishing poles. I reflected that the remains of last summer's picnics already were sealed beneath a deposit of mud, perhaps for future generations of scholars to find.

Other open-air settlements, far from the areas of rock-shelters and caves, stretched to the east across Europe. At Dolni Vestonice, 25 miles south of Brno, Czechoslovakia, archeologists discovered unexpected artifacts and the remains of a striking individual who had lived perhaps 25,000 years ago. Several huts built both of rocks and the bones of mammoths once stood at Dolni Vestonice. Mammoths had wintered nearby, and hunters apparently sought the young ones, for the bones of more than 50 immature beasts lay piled in a deep gully.

Up the slope from this settlement was a single hut. In it scholars found the earliest known oven and more than 2,000 pieces of fired clay, many of them whole or broken figurines of animals. Not far away was a grave.

A female with a disfigured face had been tenderly buried on her left side, with both hands clutching an arctic fox. Before closing the grave, her mourners had respectfully covered her body with a layer of red ocher. Two shoulder blades from a mammoth, one incised with a series of lines, were placed on top of her. Nearby were found two intriguing pieces of Ice Age art—a sculpted ivory female head and a woman's face carved on an ivory tablet. Both images showed a paralysis of the left side of the face caused by a damaged nerve, the same malady that afflicted the mysterious female. In life her face must have drooped hideously. Who was she? What had been her role in the community? We can only wonder.

Archeologist Walter A. Fairservis, Jr., (Continued on page 24)

Jumping horse transforms an 11-inch-long bone spear-thrower into a work of art. The development of this tool late in the Ice Age markedly increased hunting prowess. Hardy and resilient, Ice Age people probably had an intelligence equal to our own.

JEAN VERTUT, MUSÉE DES ANTIQUITÉS NATIONALES, ST.-GERMAIN-EN-LAYE, ORIGINALLY PUBLISHED IN "PRÉHISTOIRE DE L'ART OCCIDENTAL," BY ANDRÉ LEROI-GOURHAN © ÉDITIONS D'ART LUCIEN MAZENOD, PARIS, 1965

Haven to mankind for thousands of years, bluffs above the Vézère valley still protect cliff dwellers (below, left). The Musée National de Préhistoire, nestled in a rock-shelter, looms above a row of vine-decked houses built with the rock as their rear walls. Visitors (below, right) walk across the museum terrace, overlooking the Vézère. Once a medieval fortress, the museum now houses a treasure of Ice Age artifacts recovered from nearby sites. Curator Jean Guichard and his archeologist wife, Genevieve, (left) display stone tools and weapons from

ALL BY ROBERT FRESON

the nearby cave and rock-shelter of La Ferrassie; all came from one square meter of excavation. Charts on the table record the position of each artifact at the time of its discovery. Because of such meticulous research, each retains its important niche in the saga of Upper Paleolithic man.

21

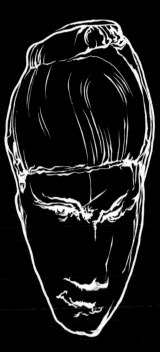

World's earliest known portrait, a carving in mammoth-tusk ivory (above) depicts a woman with a disfigured face. Archeologists found the two-inch-long carving at an Ice Age habitation site in Czechoslovakia, not far from a grave that yielded the skeleton of a woman whose skull revealed the effect of the same facial distortion. A drawing (right) shows her from the front. Scholars wonder if, because of the malady, people in her group may have considered her magical, and honored her image after her death. A faceless woman sculpted from stone (left) once decorated the wall of the rock-shelter of Laussel near Les Eyzies. The 18-inch-high figure, which may represent a fertility goddess, holds a horn incised with 13 lines. Pockmarked in a sinuous pattern, a nearly four-inch-long piece of bone (below) found in the rock-shelter of Blanchard in France may have recorded the passage of days or the cycles of the moon.

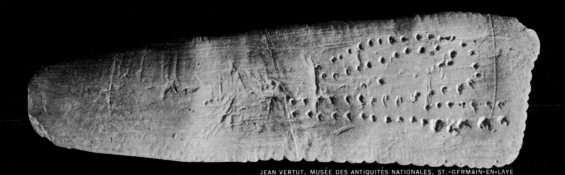

of New York's American Museum of Natural History wrote, ". . . the people of Dolni Vestonice were under constant stress owing to cold, danger, disease, food needs, and a sense of powerlessness in a world where the supernatural was all-powerful." According to Fairservis, "The woman of Dolni Vestonice with her crooked face and special burial suggests that she was regarded with certain ritual awe in life, which continued after death. Was she given to strange actions in keeping with her abnormal look? Actions which proclaimed her supernatural contacts and abilities? One cannot know, of course, but at the same time one can be reasonably sure that in the eyes of the inhabitants of ancient Dolni Vestonice she was no ordinary woman."

Whoever she was, she is still with us in the world's first known portrait. She has a pensive face, with hair upswept; her features, even the distorted ones, seem to have been carved with tenderness.

As I looked deeper into the lives of the people in my most distant past, I encountered still more mysteries. At Dolni Vestonice and other ancient campsites from the Atlantic to Siberia, female figurines played a prominent but unexplained role. They are small, often faceless, with large sagging breasts, corpulent buttocks, and rotund abdomens.

Most are naked. Some wear only jewelry. Many appear to be pregnant. Their discoverers dubbed them "Venus" figurines and suggested that they may have been fertility fetishes. Professor Fairservis points out that ". . . the problems of childbearing were apparently often fatal in one way or another." These obese Venuses, then, may have been used in fertility rites to aid in the propagation of the band and to invoke good health for mothers and infants. If so, this belief must have stretched the width of Europe. Many archeologists believe the figurines could be the basis for fertility goddesses found in European cultures and civilizations for thousands of years afterward. Yet we cannot be certain.

One conviction had begun to penetrate my thoughts. These ancient hunters must have had an intelligence as fully developed as ours. They searched for answers to the natural mysteries that surrounded them. Their interest in the world and the universe has been expounded recently by Alexander Marshack, a research associate with Harvard University's Peabody Museum.

Enigmatic markings on pieces of bone and antler long had puzzled scientists. But Marshack, after examining the artifacts with a microscope, offered an innovative interpretation. The marks apparently had not been made all at once, but over a long period of time with different tools. After studying the groups of marks, Marshack proposed that they could be a record of lunar cycles. If this is true, the markings may have been an early calendar system.

Most scholars agree with Marshack that the Ice Age hunters used the marking system to count something, but they disagree on what was being recorded. Some think it may have been related to astronomical observations. Others theorize that it was simply a way to mark the passage of days.

Archeologists have wondered why mathematics, astronomy, and the making of calendars seemed to have appeared thousands of

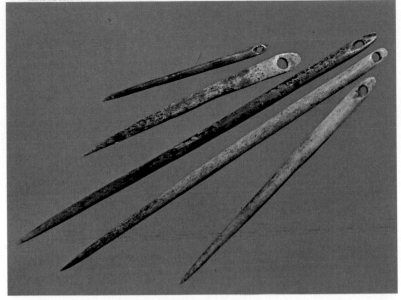

Bone needles, the longest measuring four inches, give clues to Ice Age man's survival. Probably using sinew as thread, people stitched hides into tents and windbreaks and sewed skins and furs into cloaks, tunics, trousers, caps, and shoes. Shells and beads often decorated the clothing.

years after the Ice Age. Perhaps we are now gaining clues that these fields of study had their roots with Ice Age people. If they were preoccupied with time, it may have been because of their awareness of the cycles of the seasons, an awareness that is apparent in their art.

They painted and engraved the walls of more than 110 caves from France and Spain to the Ural Mountains, and they made sculptures by the thousand. Marshack notes that "... artists realistically rendered more than fifty species of animals and plants documenting their mixed ecology, often depicting the appearance, sex, age, and the seasonal or sexual behavior of the species."

Much of their art portrays spring and summer. There are representations of animals shedding winter coats, of seals pursuing salmon upstream, of plants sprouting tender shoots, of a pair of reindeer nuzzling, of grasses growing to full seed. Life and fertility seem to whirl around the observer. Men with spears wound a bison. A woman gives birth. A man makes music with a mouth bow. Women with arms upraised appear to be at prayer. A person, possibly a priest, lifts his feet in a sprightly dance.

To create these lively and beautiful works, the artists used flint tools or sought out pigments, ground them to fine powder, and perhaps mixed them with animal fat or even egg white. Then, with torches or oil lamps, they entered the blackest chambers of the caves. They built scaffolding and began their artistic tasks.

Scholars have long wondered why these people went to such great effort. Many once agreed that it must have been for hunting magic, to keep the herds nearby. But the animals painted were not necessarily those hunted for food. French archeologist André Leroi-Gourhan has studied the art for many years, and he believes that the paintings had sexual and fertility meanings. Others suggest they are simply art for art's sake. Human beings from earliest times have had an aesthetic drive to create and to be surrounded by beauty.

25

"I believe they were designed to relieve stress," Martin Wobst told me. "They acted as reminders of past catastrophes such as starvation or natural disaster. Perhaps painting animal scenes somehow relieved the artists' anxieties about the possible reoccurrence of such catastrophes. Remember, these people had led an insecure existence during a long, unstable span of centuries. They must have suffered mass starvation at times when herd migration patterns changed."

Art Spiess thinks the paintings and sculptures served another purpose. "They seem to me to be memory cues, seasonally oriented reminders for recounting legends and telling stories appropriate to that particular time."

Whatever their purpose, I was haunted by the simple fact that these early artists used the most mysterious of the physical locales of their domain. They went deep into the earth where light never penetrates and nothing grows. For inexplicable reasons, they chose to decorate such dark recesses with flowing symbols of life from the sunlit earth.

Seasons and cycles turned once again in our modern world, and I returned to Europe in early spring, still seeking answers to questions that often remained unformed. The area of Les Eyzies had changed dramatically. Buds as delicate as whispers showed pale against the dark branches of trees. A white mist rode the Vézère and softened the stark gray cliffs. Buttercups nestled in the thickening grass. The air smelled of lilacs.

Claude Archambeau welcomed André Bousquet and me again to Les Combarelles. Again I followed them through the narrow passageways to pause at now familiar engravings of people and animals. I asked Claude why some surfaces remained untouched while others were crowded with figures superimposed one upon another. He simply shrugged.

In answer to my next question, Claude said, "The thing that impresses me most about the engravings is the great difficulty the artists had in doing them. This floor has been lowered recently by several feet. Before that, people had to crawl through small holes to reach some areas. And the artists would have had to carry lights, tools, and other equipment. Yet they returned again and again for centuries to carve the hard stone with nothing more than flint tools."

The cave of Font-de-Gaume, also near Les Eyzies, is as wide and spacious as Les Combarelles is narrow and low. Most of the art there was painted rather than engraved. I joined several other pilgrims on a long climb up the steep cliffside path that leads to the entrance. Just inside the cave, the moist stone walls sparkled as if covered with ice, reflecting light like tiny diamonds. Farther inside, the light yielded to total darkness.

Several flashlights played across the walls, and suddenly a large painted bison sprang to life. Its head bowed, it seemed to be charging at a dead run. Others near it also surged forward, and together they formed a single, powerful herd. When newly painted, these great beasts must have coursed across the walls in swaying torchlight as voices recounted epic tales. The flashlights flickered off, and I paused for a few moments in the inky blackness. I reflected that I was deep within one of the hidden chambers of the Ice Age artists; eerily, I felt their presence.

Engulfed by the darkness, I speculated on what ancient rites the people might have performed in such caves. Why had they come to these havens of blackness? Some had raked their fingers across the damp clay ceilings to make long curving lines. Even small children had placed handprints on the walls as if to say, "I am here, and am leaving a mark of my passing."

In a cave near Niaux, France, is a circle of heel prints left in clay. What were the people doing? Dancing in some forgotten ritual? We know they made music. Bone flutes capable of producing an octave of sound were found in Czechoslovakia, and a site in the Ukraine yielded percussion instruments made from mammoth bones.

And what was the meaning of the strange gridlike patterns painted on some cave walls? Authorities can say no more than that they were symbols of something. In Gönnersdorf, Germany, south of Bonn, a tent village of horse hunters was uncovered, and some 1,000 slate plaques engraved with strange symbols and dancing figures turned up. What purpose could they have served? No one knows.

I have often wondered what masterpieces these artists might have fashioned from wood or other perishable materials long since lost to the world. Yet snowflakes, among the most fragile and fleeting of nature's wonders, that fell during the winters of the Ice Age still exist. They lie locked deep within northern glaciers in the form of ice. Perhaps somewhere on the earth are locked more clues to the understanding of the Ice Age hunters.

One afternoon in his home in Les Eyzies, André Bousquet had opened a glass-front cabinet and spread a collection of stone tools and weapons on a table before me. I picked up a crude stone knife, a type I knew had been made in the beginning centuries of modern man—about 37,000 years ago during the Upper Paleolithic, the last part of the Old Stone Age. In the other hand, I held a small sharp flint blade dating from more than 27,000 years later. One weapon may have been used to help kill a mammoth, the other to butcher smaller game in the period after the earth had warmed and the mammoth had become extinct. That day I held the span of Ice Age hunters in the palms of my hands, and I felt a stirring of understanding.

Despite many unanswered questions, my journey had been rewarding. I had looked into the faces of these people, and I had seen their handiwork. I had dreamed beside the rushing Vézère, protected from winter storms by the brooding dark cliffs that had sheltered them. I had explored their caves, watched their stars, seen their moon wax to fullness and wane again.

And what had I learned of them? I had discovered that they were great hunters, carvers, painters, and musicians. They were probably makers of myths and tellers of tales. Perhaps they recited poems and sang. Perhaps they prayed.

They had become real people to me, these earliest ancestors of mine, and I felt that it would not be strange to know them. Yet their mysterious story remains largely untold, and the secrets of their inner souls elude me still.

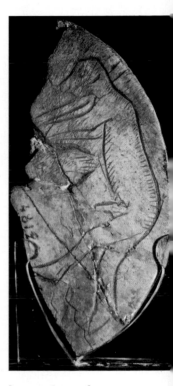

Bewildering tableau: An animal-man, or a man wearing an animal mask, dances spiritedly on a fragment of a bone disk found in a cave in France. He shoulders a large pole as a huge bear paw stretches toward him. Its meaning unclear, the disk may illustrate a long-forgotten religious rite, a heroic struggle, or perhaps a mystical tale of beasts and sorcerers.

JEAN VERTUT, MUSÉE DES ANTIQUITÉS NATIONALES, ST.-GERMAIN-EN-LAYE, ORIGINALLY PUBLISHED IN "PRÉHISTOIRE DE L'ART OCCIDENTAL," BY ANDRÉ LEROI-GOURHAN © ÉDITIONS D'ART LUCIEN MAZENOD, PARIS, 1965

Woolly mammoths, their bulky bodies
outlined in paint, confront each other
in the cave of Rouffignac in France

Sometime before 10,000 B.C., the glaciers began to recede in Europe and the earth to warm.
Mammoths and many other large beasts of the Ice Age gradually became extinct, and man, as
he learned the rudiments of agriculture, turned from watchful hunter to settled farmer.

ROOTS OF THE CITY: JERICHO AND ÇATAL HÜYÜK

by LOUIS DE LA HABA

photographed by NATHAN BENN

Down from the heights of Jerusalem through barren hills etched against a cloudless sky, down twenty-five hundred feet to a sign marked "Sea Level," I drove under the scorching sun of a Middle Eastern spring. Down almost another thousand feet, past an occasional Arab sheltering with his camel in the uncertain shade of a sparsely leafed tree, I entered the valley of the River Jordan and a verdant oasis filled with flowers and orchards. This was Arīḫā, the Arabic name for Jericho, a thriving community on the Israeli-occupied west bank of the Jordan.

A mile northwest of the town, at a spring near the Mount of Temptation—where Jesus is said to have struggled with the Devil—rises a dusty, oval mound. In Arabic it is called Tell es Sultan, and it is the site of ancient Jericho. Near the top of the mound, long since eroded by wind and rain, once stood walls that, according to the Old Testament, fell to Joshua's trumpets some time around 1250 B.C. Near the bottom, exposed in a trench dug by archeologists, are other walls built nearly 7,000 years before Joshua lived, walls of stone that hold tantalizing clues to the early people of Jericho. These residents, who may have numbered about 2,500, built the first known permanent community. They built it during Neolithic times—the last phase of the Stone Age—when Ice Age hunters of France and Spain were leaving their rock-shelters and seeking to adapt to new ways of life in a changing environment.

The huge animals of the glacial wilds that had sustained those

Overleaf: With haunting stares, skulls peer from ten thousand years in the past. Uncovered at Jericho, site of the world's oldest known community, the skulls have features molded in plaster and eyes made of seashells. Scholars theorize that the people of Jericho worshiped the skulls of ancestors. About 9000 B.C., in the Neolithic, or New Stone Age, many people in the Middle East (right) began to gather into communities—for protection, to utilize permanent water sources, or because of the settling influences of farming and herding.

AMMAN ARCHAEOLOGICAL MUSEUM
(OVERLEAF)

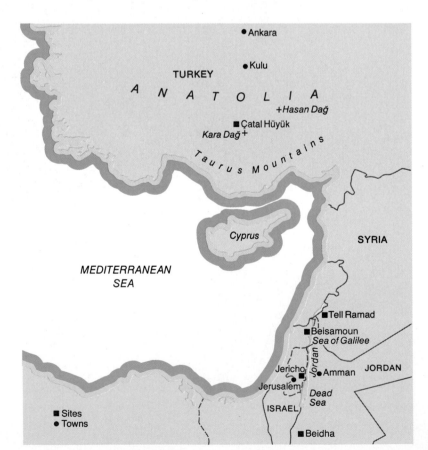

hunters, such as mammoths, had become extinct or had moved northward with the receding ice sheets. In the warmer climate following the Ice Age, woodlands and grasslands gradually replaced glaciers, and the people stalked smaller game—boar, deer, horses, and cattle. They gathered berries, nuts, honey, and wild-grain ancestors of wheat and barley. They may have tamed the dog, as guard and hunting companion. Much later, exactly when remains obscure, they domesticated sheep, goats, and cattle, and learned to plant seeds: wheat and other cereals, lentils and other legumes.

When the first Neolithic people settled in Jericho, they already knew agriculture. A sign of this is the presence in the mound's debris of flint-edged sickles for cutting grain and of stone querns in which to grind it. As yet these people had no pottery.

There is evidence of even earlier people at Jericho, people who had made their campsites at the spring, perhaps seasonally, perhaps permanently. Some scholars believe that it could have been these who became the first town dwellers, at first hunting and foraging in the oasis and later—somehow—obtaining the basic, yet revolutionary, knowledge of plant propagation. Others contend that the first builders of Jericho may have been newcomers who brought the seeds and the knowledge with them.

In either case, locals or outsiders, they possessed the seeds of civilization. Here they planted them. Here the people grew in number, prospered, and built their town, here in this place by the spring.

Today, that spring, the Biblical Fountain of Elisha, bubbles from beneath a concrete enclosure. Pumps propel its waters to Arīḥā, where they nurture the soil of gardens and orchards. I walked to the spring and dipped my hands into its crystal coolness, as people must have done for untold ages. Then I climbed to the top of Jericho.

This 70-foot-high mound is an artificial hill built up by successive periods of human occupation, each new layer erected upon the ruins of the old. It covers about eight acres. North and east of the mound thousands of empty dwellings, mud-walled and square, make patterns of light and shadow in the harsh sunlight. These had been the houses of Palestinian refugees who have since moved on. But that is an unfinished part of modern history.

The mound of Jericho holds another unfinished story, the story of urban man and how this form of civilization, so universal in our time, first came about.

Within one trench dug deep into the heart of Tell es Sultan rises a massive round tower, a mystifying structure built of stone by the first Neolithic inhabitants. Gingerly treading the dry and crumbly edges of the trench, I stepped across to the tower's flat top. There, squeezing through a sort of hatch, I entered the darkness of a steeply sloping stairway and squirmed down 22 stone steps. Finally, I crawled on all fours through a narrow opening and came out into the burning, breathless air of the shadowless trench. I was now at a level archeologists have dated at about 8000 B.C. Because no pottery was found there, archeologists have given it the unwieldy name of Pre-Pottery Neolithic A, or PPNA. A silty layer representing some 500 years of abandonment separates this level from the next. This one also lacks pottery and has been designated as PPNB; it dates to the seventh millennium B.C. Another layer of silting that lasted several centuries separates the PPNB layer from the next, another Neolithic phase in which pottery shards and artifacts suddenly appear. And above, starting at about 3000 B.C., are the eroded Bronze Age and later levels. Behind me stood the tower—it would have seemed more at home in medieval Europe, I thought—and part of a wall.

Excavations of Neolithic Jericho were carried out from 1952 until 1958 by the late Kathleen M. Kenyon, a British archeologist who was created a Dame of the Order of the British Empire in recognition of her work.

I met Dame Kathleen in London a few months before her death in August 1978. She told me of her surprise when walls and a tower began to emerge under the spades of her crew. The structures bespoke a level of organization and a degree of sophistication in construction until then unsuspected for the Neolithic.

Dame Kathleen believed the walls were built for defensive purposes. But to her they remained a mystery. "A mystery because we don't know from whom the people of Jericho wanted to defend themselves. It may have been that the spring was so valuable that other people who were still leading a wandering life were sufficiently jealous to try to raid it."

The spring, of course, and the fertile land around it must have been the reasons people decided to settle in Jericho. Anyone who has experienced the barrenness of the surrounding desert can have little doubt of that. Jericho must have seemed a most desirable place.

But at least one archeologist has an alternative to Dame Kathleen's explanation for the walls. I talked with Professor Ofer Bar-Yosef in his office at the Hebrew University in Jerusalem. He had just come from a tour of nighttime reserve duty with the Israeli Army. Where Dr. Kenyon found evidence of fortifications and warfare, Professor Bar-Yosef sees something else.

"Every few kilometers along the Jordan Valley you will find a wadi, a usually dry streambed, that carries runoff of winter rains down from the mountains. This runoff brings down silt that forms alluvial fans at the mouths of the wadis. People cultivated these alluvial fans because they were fertile, being replenished each year by fresh deposits of soil.

"Now, let's say you're a Neolithic farmer living in Jericho. If you don't want to be flooded and silted over, the only way to prevent this is by building a wall. I believe that silting and wall building were parts of the same phenomenon. As the silting increased, people raised the walls higher, or built new ones. I would argue that protection against flooding and silting is a much better reason for the walls than warfare," he said.

As corroborating evidence, he mentioned other Neolithic sites in the Jordan Valley that, without walls, were eventually engulfed by silt. And he cited Beidha, a Neolithic village in Jordan that had a terrace wall and did not suffer silting.

"Even with the annual renewal of the soil," Professor Bar-Yosef continued, "I would assume that after a while, and especially after droughts, the alluvial fans would become exhausted. So probably

Bone implements from Jericho, used for sewing and weaving, rest in the hollow of the spatula-like leg bone of an animal (opposite). An artist in Jericho fashioned a smiling plaster bust, perhaps a stylistic development from the earlier plastered skulls. Like the skulls, the head has seashells inserted into its sockets to represent eyes. Incised lines signify hair and a beard.

what the people did was simply move to another place to farm. This would explain something that has always been bizarre in Neolithic stratigraphy. Nowhere do we have in one mound continuous evidence of settlement—we have no more than a few hundred years, then an interruption. I strongly suggest that exhaustion of the soil is an explanation for the 500-year gap between PPNA and PPNB levels."

Whatever the reason for the walls, the purpose of the tower also is unexplained. "It could be a watchtower," Dame Kathleen told me, "but that depends, you see, on whether it's a single one, or one of several. If there are more than one, then they would be normal military affairs. If it's the only one, then I would say it was the stronghold of a leader. Beside it there are storage tanks, one lot for water and the other lot probably for grain. I do just toy with the idea that the tower may have belonged to the king, or mayor, or whatever, who was sort of keeping control of his own special source of supplies."

Because Jericho has been only partially excavated, there is no way of telling, at the moment, just how far the walls extend or how many towers there may have been.

Professor Bar-Yosef told me he could only theorize about the reasons for the tower. He suggested it might even have been the base of a device for lifting water from storage tanks and emptying it into irrigation channels. "Anyway," he concluded, "it remains enigmatic."

But then, so does almost everything else at Jericho. The skulls, for example.

I saw them at the Amman Archaeological Museum in Jordan and held one in my hands with an eerie sense of awe, for I was looking not at bare bone, but at the full face of a Neolithic man. These are no ordinary skulls. Laboriously, perhaps lovingly, someone long ago had plastered them over, restoring the facial features—nose, cheeks, ears, and eyes. Seashells inserted in the eye sockets gave the skulls a living, knowing look. Similar skulls have been found at other sites of roughly the same period—notably at Beisamoun, north of the Sea of Galilee, and at Tell Ramad in Syria. Other unplastered but sometimes painted skulls have been found throughout the Middle East as far away as Turkey. Scholars have speculated on the existence of skull cults in these areas.

"From this treatment of the skulls," Dr. Kenyon wrote in her book *Digging Up Jericho*, "it may be deduced that these early inhabitants . . . had already developed a conception of a spiritual life. . . . They must have felt that some power, perhaps protective, perhaps of wisdom, would survive death, and somehow they must have realised that the seat of these extracorporeal powers was the head. They perhaps believed that the preservation of the skull secured the use of the power to succeeding generations, perhaps that it placated the spirit, perhaps controlled it."

Professor Bar-Yosef sees territorial-political implications in the treatment of the skulls. "The cult of the ancestors means that you demonstrate to yourself, to your neighbors, to the people of the community, the continuity of your rights in the area. Don't you think that recent political problems have something (Continued on page 41)

AMMAN ARCHAEOLOGICAL MUSEUM (TOP); COURTESY ISRAEL DEPARTMENT OF ANTIQUITIES AND MUSEUMS, EXHIBITED AT THE ROCKEFELLER MUSEUM, JERUSALEM

Guardian of the past, the mound of ancient Jericho rises between the greenery of the modern town and the abandoned houses of a Palestinian refugee camp. In the distance, a dull gray line marks the bitter waters of the Dead Sea. Archeologist Dame Kathleen Kenyon (left), Jericho's principal excavator, works in the study of her home in Wales three months before her death in

August 1978. A trench dug in the 1950's under Dr. Kenyon's supervision revealed large storage bins for food and water next to a round stone tower (above, right) some 30 feet high and 30 feet in diameter. From the base of the tower, 22 narrow stone steps (right) lead to an opening at the top. The purpose of the tower, which dates to about 8000 B.C., remains a mystery. A watchtower? Part of Jericho's defenses? The stronghold of a ruler? No one can say with certainty. Archeologists found many levels of construction at Jericho, but no trace of the walls that Joshua destroyed.

Effigies of four bulls and a ram—considered male fertility symbols—dominate the wall of a shrine from Çatal Hüyük in Turkey. Reconstructed, the shrine today stands in the Museum of Anatolian Civilizations in Ankara. More than 40 such shrines came to light at Çatal Hüyük, excavated under the direction of James Mellaart (left), now of the University of London. Mellaart estimates that more than 5,000 people worked and lived in Çatal Hüyük's densely clustered mud-walled houses between 6500 and 5700 B.C. On a sun-drenched morning, the site's overseer walks past the ruins (below). Mellaart excavated only one of the city's thirty-two acres. Archeologists at Çatal Hüyük

discovered pottery and stone artifacts, the world's first known paintings on man-made walls, and indications of an economy based on agriculture, trade, and manufacture. Rich religious imagery suggests the city may have served as a spiritual center.

to do with old traditions in the Middle East, that everyone feels that this is his country and that he is attached to it psychologically?''

Territorial or ritual, the plastered skulls do not appear in Jericho until the PPNB, and this is another of the site's unplumbed secrets. Who were the PPNB people? Were they, as Professor Bar-Yosef theorizes, descendants of the original inhabitants who returned to dimly remembered ancestral lands? Or were they a second wave of immigrants, as Dame Kathleen thought, possibly from northern Syria? And what of the newcomers who settled Jericho centuries after the PPNB people, bringing with them a full-scale pottery industry, yet building houses that were rude in comparison with the architecture of much earlier times? The answers are a matter for conjecture.

If Jericho remains an enigma, another Old World Neolithic site is an enigma within a mystery. The mound of Çatal Hüyük slopes gently upward from a field in the fertile Konya Plain, Turkey's wheat-growing region on the Anatolian Plateau. The site lays a strong claim to being the oldest true city in the world. Apparently it was a religious and trade center, with an economy based on agriculture, manufacture, and trade in raw and finished products. Although only one of its thirty-two acres has been excavated extensively, the community's population has been estimated at upwards of 5,000 people, based on the size of the site and the densely clustered houses in it.

While Çatal flourished, between 6500 and 5700 B.C., it must have presented a strange aspect. Solid mud-brick walls faced the outsider. As with the pueblos of the American Southwest, the houses of Çatal Hüyük were entered from the roofs. The individual buildings usually had no common walls but were built hard against one another, and the inhabitants had to walk across others' roofs to reach their own quarters, which they entered by means of wooden ladders.

In the early morning of an Anatolian autumn, archeologists have imagined, a Neolithic visitor to Çatal Hüyük might have witnessed scenes such as these:

Farmers emerge from the city to harvest plots planted in wheat, barley, and peas. Herders come out to look after cattle, only recently domesticated. Groups of hunters set out toward the distant Taurus Mountains in search of wild boar and deer; the men wear leopard-skin loincloths, and their bodies are painted red, black, or both in a harlequin pattern. Down the river that flows across the plain from the wooded Taurus, men float rafts of timber for the frameworks of new houses in the growing city. And from snowcapped mountains far to the northeast, traders arrive with bags of obsidian—volcanic glass—which capable artisans of Çatal will fashion into a catalog of Neolithic artifacts: knives, spearheads, arrow points; tools for working wood, bone, and leather; sickles; and obsidian mirrors into which women will peer as they daintily apply red ocher to their faces with small bone spatulas.

In the city, men repair roofs and replaster walls to protect them from snowstorms in the coming winter. Women grind grain or tend hearths. On the newly plastered wall of a shrine, an artist paints a hunting scene. In another shrine, a priestess places an offering of last

Grotesquely obese yet awesomely imperious, Çatal Hüyük's mother goddess sits between two felines—possibly lions. The figure, in the act of giving birth, symbolizes the goddess's mastery over life—human and animal. Archeologists found the eight-inch-high clay figure, now partly reconstructed, in the grain bin of a shrine; people of Çatal Hüyük may have placed it there to promote bountiful crops.

41

year's grain before the statuette of an obese mother goddess. She believes, as do all of Çatal's people, that this will continue to ensure a bountiful harvest. To still another shrine, a procession of people solemnly carries the skeleton of a departed leader from a charnel house where vultures have stripped it of flesh. They will bury the skeleton beneath a platform, with cowrie shells from the distant Red Sea placed in its eye sockets.

Çatal Hüyük hums with activity. Its innovative residents work with metals, engage in widespread trade, irrigate fields, decorate homes and shrines with marvelous paintings, and do all sorts of things they're not supposed to be doing—at least according to the archeology of the pre-1960's.

But Çatal Hüyük revolutionized the traditional view of Neolithic times when James Mellaart, now of the University of London, began excavations there in 1961. The memories of that first season are as vivid as yesterday in Mellaart's mind.

"We went into an area where we'd seen mud bricks, splinters of bone, broken arrowheads, bits of pottery, and so on," he told me as he puffed on a cigar in his London office. "The first day produced nothing but rather crummy walls and lots of ashes. There was no doubt, though, that it was Neolithic. Then, on the third day, one of my men, working in a very narrow trench, banged his shovel against a wall. A bit of plaster fell off, and below it was a great red patch. We peeled off the outer layer of plaster and found our first wall painting—it was a hunting scene. After that, of course, we knew we were in clover. We were positive that the site was going to produce many, many interesting things."

And so it did.

Mellaart and his excavators uncovered a staggering wealth of materials from Çatal Hüyük. Of these, the paintings were the biggest surprise, and are among the most intriguing of Çatal's many mysteries. They appear mostly in buildings that seem to be religious shrines. Some of them cover entire walls, sometimes spilling around a corner onto a second wall. Bold in color and design, they depict hunting scenes full of life and motion, scenes of games in which men tease and dance around bulls and stags, grisly scenes of vultures pecking at headless bodies—all done in strong reds, yellows, blacks, and flesh-tone pinks.

One painting may be the world's oldest landscape, and perhaps qualifies as the first news picture. In it, a double peak spews smoke and flames, and shoots a shower of volcanic bombs into the air. At its foot a geometric design of connected oblongs resembles a town plan. There are no such volcanoes in the immediate vicinity of Çatal Hüyük, but Hasan Dağ thrusts its jagged crest above the plain some 80 miles to the northeast, and Kara Dağ's ragged silhouette is clearly visible 25 miles to the southeast. Both are volcanoes that may have been active in Neolithic times.

The meaning of other paintings is obscure, although Mellaart thinks of them as ritual in nature. In the concept and execution of the hunting scenes, he detects stylistic ties with the cave paintings of Ice Age Europe. And in the paintings of bulls he can visualize the games and rituals so prevalent thousands of years later in Minoan Crete. But at this point in our knowledge of Anatolian prehistory, these links are too tenuous to trace.

Because many of the paintings were plastered over and never repainted, Mellaart thinks they "were made in connection with certain events the precise nature of which we shall probably never ascertain. Çatal Hüyük is, however, one of those rare cases in archeology where man tried to communicate some of his thoughts. For us to read them is another matter."

Today the site of Çatal Hüyük is a magnificent shambles. The excavations in the 55-foot-high mound are like open wounds in its grassy flank. Although remains of walls expose their brick construction, most of the area is covered by weeds, raspy-leafed succulents the Turks call "mother-in-law tongues," and wild flowers in patches of purple, blue, yellow, and blood red.

In one side of the excavation I saw, in lengthwise section, part of the cranium, ribs, and leg bones of a Neolithic child, slightly more than four feet tall. Excavators at Çatal Hüyük unearthed hundreds of skeletons from beneath the platforms, altars, and floors of many houses and shrines.

From them, Dr. J. Lawrence Angel of the Smithsonian Institution in Washington, D. C., has determined that Çatal's male adults averaged 5 feet 7 inches in height, and that females averaged 5 feet 1$\frac{1}{2}$ inches, that they had an adequate diet, and that many suffered from anemia perhaps caused by malaria. Adult average age at time of death was slightly more than 34 years for men and just under 30 for women—about two years older than the earlier Upper Paleolithic populations. Dr. Angel has suggested that the increase in longevity is responsible for the rapid population growth at Çatal, the additional years allowing women more time for childbearing.

"The reason for this vital advance in lifespan for females . . . seems obvious. It was the completely settled and relatively secure life of the trading settlement. . . ," Dr. Angel has reported.

In this secure setting the women of Çatal Hüyük may well have held a position of great importance. Certainly the central deity in Çatal religion was a woman. Female statuettes abound, some roughly carved from stalactites imported from far-off mountain caves, others artfully modeled in clay. In the shrines, along with such male symbols as bull and ram heads and altars decorated with the actual horn cores of bulls, also appear reliefs of a mother goddess. Quite possibly Çatal Hüyük's religious life centered on female fertility and was directed by priestesses.

Felines also played a prominent role. Two animals, possibly lions, flank the most important representation of the earth mother yet found at Çatal Hüyük—a commanding, seated woman with protruding breasts and belly. In some of the shrines, pairs of leopards in relief appear facing each other. Unlike the paintings, the reliefs were repainted when plastered over, the design of the spots varying with each new version.

Most of the objects excavated from Çatal Hüyük are on exhibit in the Museum of Anatolian Civilizations in Ankara. There I saw evidence of the wealth of the city and of the skill and imagination of its artisans: finely flaked obsidian and flint weapons, polished stone axes and bowls, rings, pendants, and bead necklaces made of stone, of shell, and—most surprisingly for a Stone Age site—of copper and lead. Some of the paintings, carefully removed from the site with their plaster and mud-brick backings, faded badly after their once-bright colors were exposed to light and air. Experts are attempting to restore many of them.

As in some of the cave art of the Upper Paleolithic, a few of the Çatal Hüyük paintings show human hands as part of the total design or as border motifs. In one display case I saw a collection of small, rectangular bones. I recognized them as animal bones and wondered about their significance.

Raci Temizer, director of the museum, told me that they were sheep astragali—ankle bones—and were used as pieces for a game that, as he described it, must have combined elements of both marbles and dice.

"Boys in Anatolia still play with astragali," Dr. Temizer said. "Today, they call the game aşik, but it's basically the same one played thousands of years ago. Here you can see the importance of continuity in Anatolian prehistory. The hands on the Çatal Hüyük paintings are another example. Even today villagers often paint hands on their houses, or make hand imprints when they replaster outside walls. It's for good luck."

J ericho and Çatal Hüyük are incomplete though hugely informative bridges that have helped span gaps in the long prehistory of the Middle East—and of mankind. But, because of the incomplete nature of the excavations, many questions remain unanswered about both sites and the people who lived there, about their religion, their form of government, their trade networks, and their relationships with one another.

At Çatal Hüyük, for example, the excavated area is clearly a religious quarter. It seems improbable that the entire city would have consisted of shrines and houses of the wealthy. Where were the workshops for flint and obsidian and stone? Where were the markets, the cattle corrals, the storage areas for crops? Even in the excavated area, down to some 15 feet below the present level of the plain, the lowest layer of human occupation has not been reached. So information about Çatal's origins is still lacking.

At Jericho, there are the walls and those unexplained gaps in occupation about which archeologists can only guess. And the skull cult: How did this idea spread among people so diverse and distant as the inhabitants of Çatal Hüyük and Jericho?

Çatal Hüyük has not been worked since 1965; digging at Jericho stopped in 1958. At present there are no plans for further excavation at either site.

What treasures still lie hidden within the mounds one cannot begin to imagine. Without a doubt, new finds would answer many of the questions that still puzzle archeologists. But also without a doubt, new finds would give rise to further mysteries about these earliest urban centers of mankind.

Ankle bones of sheep (above), called astragali, serve as pieces in a game played in Turkey since Neolithic times. Archeologists found these bones in the ruins of Çatal Hüyük. A boy in the Anatolian village of Kulu prepares to toss a similar bone on the ground. Players score points according to which side of the bone lands upright, a system that resembles—and may have led to—modern dice games.

44

ud-brick houses of Çatal Hüyük command
Turkey's Konya Plain on an autumn day in
this re-creation based on the work of James

Mellaart. Herders lead cattle toward a river that may have flowed nearby. A woman places grapes on a kilim—a colorful woven rug—to dry in the sun; others spread winnowed wheat and barley. Using slingshots, boys try to fell a crane. Their friends play a game with sheep bones.

Plaster leopards (below) face each other on the wall of a Çatal Hüyük shrine. A common religious motif, the leopards may represent the mother goddess, whom they often accompany. Neolithic artists replastered and repainted these animals 40 times, sometimes leaving them white, but more often painting their spots in ever-changing patterns.

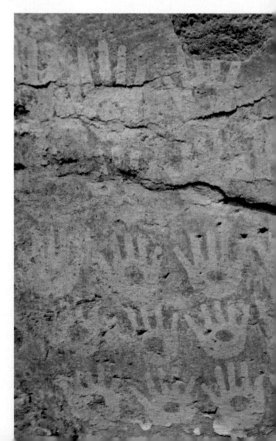

NATHAN BENN (BELOW, LEFT); OTHERS BY ARLETTE MELLAART AND IAN TODD

Wildly gesticulating celebrants dance around a huge bull (above) in a mural by an unknown artist. The painting, one of many at Çatal Hüyük, decorated the wall of a shrine. Although some of the men, dressed in leopard skins, carry bows and spears, the painting shows a joyful game rather than a hunt. Only two other Neolithic sites—Bouqras in Syria and Umm Dabaghiyah in Iraq—have yielded wall paintings, but neither of the quality and complexity of the ones at Çatal Hüyük. Images of human hands (left) appear in several paintings, a theme that persists in Anatolia to this day. At far left, a villager shows the impression of a hand, a symbol of good luck, above the doorway of his house.

Polished obsidian mirror, perhaps owned by a highborn woman of 8,000 years ago, reflects the visage of a museum worker in Ankara. At Çatal Hüyük, women used such mirrors while applying cosmetics. With a small bone spatula (upper right), they scooped ocher, a natural pigment, from a shell holder, spread it thinly on a stone palette, and then daubed it on their faces. Excavators found delicate jewelry in many tombs, including bead necklaces of apatite (second from top). Baked clay seals (third from top) may have served

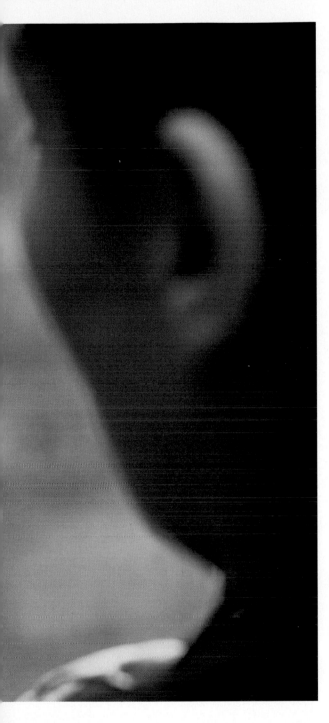

to stamp dye patterns on the skin or to apply them to cloth. Ancient fires at Çatal Hüyük carbonized most of the textiles, but the few remaining samples show skill in weaving. A young woman buried in a shrine, for instance, wore a fringed string skirt decorated with copper tubes. Bone hooks and eyes (bottom), found only in the burials of men, may have fastened garments of leopard skin.

Artistry in obsidian: Skilled craftsmen of Çatal Hüyük excelled at working the volcanic glass quarried in mountains far to the northeast.

To make the spearpoints, arrowheads, and scrapers shown here, workers carefully chipped flakes from larger pieces of the glass. Trade in raw and finished obsidian may have fueled the economy of Çatal Hüyük—one of the earliest links in the development of urban life.

EGYPT'S PYRAMIDS: MONUMENTS OF THE PHARAOHS

by TOM MELHAM

photographed by FRED MAROON

They have stood for almost 5,000 years, these man-made mountains we call pyramids. *Five thousand years*—time enough for the Roman Empire to rise and fall a dozen times over. Time, indeed, for all of Western civilization to run its course.

Long before Caesar or Pericles or even Hammurabi; before Moses and the Exodus; before Tutankhamun; before Egypt's Valley of the Kings sheltered a single royal tomb or Mesopotamia's ancient city of Nineveh began to bloom—the pyramids already were old. Yet they stand today, relatively intact despite nearly fifty centuries of earthquakes, wars, tourists, tomb robbers, neglect, and natural decay. Little wonder that they have come to symbolize eternity itself.

Millions have visited them, thousands have written about them, hundreds of archeologists have probed them. One might expect that pyramid knowledge could not be more complete.

"But they are still bewildering," says John Cooney, for 24 years the director of the Brooklyn Museum's Egypt Collection. "We've no original sources that explain how or why the pyramids were built. And there are only a few references to pyramids in any ancient Egyptian text at all. I think that's extraordinary."

Design the world's largest stone structures, labor over each for decades, and not even describe their appearance?

"Very strange," muses Cooney, "very strange indeed. In fact, if the pyramids were not physically present today, I might doubt they ever existed on so grand a scale. The ancient pyramid builders, it seems, were just not historically minded. Oh, they conquered many peoples and built enormous monuments, but they apparently never wrote out any social or political records. We don't know why. Perhaps the pyramids were so obvious that no one thought to explain them, any more than a Roman Catholic today would constantly write that St. Peter's was the head church of his faith."

Cooney adds that the pyramid form "is a curious one to choose. Four triangular faces rise from a square base to a single point high in the air. Most scholars believe that the form symbolizes a ramp or a stairway to the heavens."

Dr. Gerhard Haeny, director of the Cairo-based Swiss Institute for Architectural and Archeological Research, considers the shape "one of Egypt's greatest achievements in art, a pure geometric abstraction. You can see pyramids for miles, yet you can't judge their height at any distance because they're unadorned. They have no columns, windows, or doors that relate to the size of a man."

The reason, Haeny suggests, may lie in religious conviction.

"The ancient Greeks always built in harmony with human proportions, even in their greatest architecture—the Parthenon, for example. Their gods also were very human. But not Egyptian gods; they were far, far bigger than men. This might explain why Egypt's religious architecture ignored human scale. It was a way of saying that the gods belonged to a completely different, superior world."

Certainly an aura of otherworldliness, a brooding and slightly ominous mystique, embraces the pyramids still. Visitors have noted it for centuries. "A maddening desire to comprehend their meaning surges in the heart of the beholder," recorded a 13th-century Arab poet. Elizabeth Barrett Browning wrote of "the secret hid under Egypt's pyramid." At Giza, in the very shadow of the pyramids, Napoleon braced his troops for battle not with "La Marseillaise" but with the words, "Soldiers, forty centuries look down upon you." Even today, when the sulfurous haze of a *khamseen*, a summer dust storm, blots out the horizon and nearly all else, the pyramids' bulky profiles somehow loom through and seem to float hauntingly above. The effect is surreal, enchanting, almost alien.

But of course they are so incredibly immense. The Great Pyramid, built by the pharaoh Cheops, sprawls across 13 acres of desert, more than twice the area encompassed by Rome's Colosseum.

Two lesser triangles of limestone and granite accompany the Great Pyramid on the Giza plateau, forming the most enduring and familiar trio on earth. They are not, however, Egypt's only pyramids. Some 80 others join them on the Nile's west bank, rising up in a long and narrow artificial mountain range that borders the eastern edge of the vast Sahara. Early Greek historians dubbed the Giza pyramids the most marvelous of the ancient world's Seven Wonders. They were by far the largest and the oldest; of the original seven, they alone survive today. Most pyramids stand within 50 miles of Cairo, and most of these date from the Third through the Sixth Dynasties of Egypt's Old Kingdom, which ruled from about 2685 to 2180 B.C. To climb one of Cairo's minarets today and see those distant peaks towering above river and desert is to feel the alluring but faintly frightening tug of the unknown. What sort of people built these structures? How? Why?

Seek the answers to such questions among the ancient sources and you face a tangle of conflicting theories, fables, and wild speculations. Pliny the Younger called pyramids "a superfluous and foolish display of wealth," suggesting pharaohs erected them to exhaust the treasury and so deprive their successors. A religious writer of the 12th century considered them the Biblical granaries of Joseph, built to survive Egypt's Seven Lean Years. Medieval Arabs thought them storehouses for the wisdom and riches of a long-departed civilization. More recent theories have even described pyramids as lookout towers, landing pads for ancient astronauts, and geodetic markers used to resurvey the land after the Nile's floods.

Of all pyramids, Cheops's—the largest and most complex—always has drawn the most attention. Mathematicians of the 19th century marveled that its proportions incorporated elements of Pythagorean geometry thousands of years before Pythagoras. Other Victorians, fired by their era's fascination with all things Egyptian, left hardly a stone of this pyramid unmeasured. Doggedly, they sought some cosmic significance in its dimensions, in its precise angle of slope (51° 52'), in its location (just south of the 30th parallel on

Man-made mountain range of more than 80 pyramids crowns the west bank of the Nile for 400 miles between Abu Roash and El Kula. The largest and most lavish monuments took shape in a mere 160 years, from about 2650 to 2490 B.C., during the Old Kingdom's Third and Fourth Dynasties.

Centuries may pass, but Egypt's timeless magic endures—at Giza (left), in the rural Delta (below, left), and along the Nile, realm of graceful feluccas (below). Each of Giza's stony sentinels harbors entryways, corridors, and rooms the exact uses of which remain unclear. Dozens of theories seek to explain the pyramids on religious, mathematical, political, or other grounds. Most Egyptologists contend that each monument sheltered the body of a departed king. Another theory suggests that pharaohs used them as colossal work projects, designed to unify a disparate nation through a single purpose. Still another poses a possible astronomical role—most pyramids align with the four cardinal directions, and many passageways point to important stars.

NATIONAL GEOGRAPHIC PHOTOGRAPHER WINFIELD PARKS

FARRELL GREHAN

the meridian that bisects the Nile's delta), in its alignments with the North Pole and certain stars (some are very accurate), even in the size, shape, and direction of its shadow.

Nothing seemed too slight to ignore. Each odd fact or coincidence blossomed into a new theory. No theorist could really prove his diagnosis, but no one could absolutely disprove it, either. The result: a swarm of fantasies as numerous and persistent as Egypt's flies.

Cheops's pyramid, instead of being regarded as merely a tomb, became an astronomical observatory, a huge stone calendar, an almanac of formulas and standard measures, a squared-off scale model of earth's hemisphere proving that Egyptians knew the size and shape of the world long before Greek minds "discovered" the same knowledge. Religious fanatics interpreted the Great Pyramid as a Bible in stone, its interior passageways and rooms symbolic of the most important Scriptural events from Adam to the Apocalypse! Rudyard Kipling took a more down-to-earth approach: "Who shall doubt the secret hid/ Under Cheops' pyramid/ Is that some contractor did/ Cheops out of several millions?"

Even in today's technological age, mystics spout "pyramid power," an occult force they claim permeates pyramids, enabling them to mummify cats, to prevent food from spoiling, and to keep razor blades sharp. Rubbish, say the scientists.

Egyptian archeologist Zahi Hawass still laughs about his experience of 1976 during a lecture tour of American colleges.

"I was asked to speak on my excavations and on the pyramids, and you know at one Eastern college, five students in the front row were wearing plastic pyramids on their heads and staring straight ahead during the whole speech—one hour! I got very nervous. Later,

Enigmatic sarcophagus of King Sekhemkhet, artfully bored from a single block of alabaster and hidden deep within his unfinished pyramid, contained nothing, although its discoverers found it sealed with the original plaster. Similar intact-yet-empty coffers in other pyramids suggest these massive structures may have served as cenotaphs—funerary memorials—rather than tombs.

I learned they were meditating or something. Then at Santa Barbara, people told me that some Californians make pyramids and live inside them because they think they have magic. It's crazy!"

Nothing exasperates most Egyptologists quite so much as this sort of pyramid quackery. Says Cooney: "There are endless theories—we get a new one every year. Some people still feel that little green men in pink flying saucers came down and built the pyramids. You *can't* dissuade them. I only wish those little green men had stayed around and cleared up some of the mysteries."

Dr. I. E. S. Edwards, retired Keeper of Egyptian Antiquities at the British Museum and the leading pyramid scholar, discounts the mystics. "They are generally called 'pyramidiots.' And of course these people know absolutely nothing about the archeology of the major pyramids," he said. "These structures are royal tombs, simply one element in a whole complex of buildings, all of which were related in their funerary purpose."

Most Egyptologists today hew to this opinion, and evidence supporting it is impressive. All pyramids stand on the Nile's west bank, traditional abode of Egypt's dead; many hold, or did hold, what appear to be stone coffins; a few unidentified and undated remains have been found; thousands of proven tombs crowd around the larger pyramids like courtiers about a king. Most pyramids contain a long, sloping entryway that points north, roughly toward a group of stars that the ancients identified with the gods.

The discovery, in 1881, of a pyramid inscribed with funerary ritual further reinforced the tomb theory, but failed to provide the ultimate proof. It lacked both a royal mummy and a lavishly decorated sepulcher. The reason at first appeared (Continued on page 67)

Still running after 4,600 years, King Djoser, first to erect a stone pyramid, sprints across an inset panel (below, left) at Saqqara, in the temple complex surrounding his pyramid. Djoser's life-size statue, walled up inside a doorless cell (below), peers through a peephole—one of its two such windows on the world.

ank of stone cobras, symbolizing regal control
over Lower Egypt, braces at attention atop a
small tomb near Djoser's multi-tiered Step

Pyramid. Built at Saqqara, near the ancient capital of Memphis, this innovative structure launched Egypt's golden age of pyramid construction. Successive kings erected similar stepped monuments and, eventually, smooth-sided "true pyramids" such as those at Giza.

Two tombs for one monarch? King Snefru, *father of Cheops and founder of the dynasty that succeeded Djoser's line, broke the one-pyramid-per-pharaoh tradition by building the "Bent Pyramid" of Dahshur (above) and another one nearby—and possibly the pyramid at Meidum (right). Why so many? No one knows, but their presence causes some experts to doubt the theory that Egyptians built pyramids solely to entomb pharaohs. "Perhaps they served some religious or mystical purpose," suggests lifelong Egyptologist John Cooney (left). "We simply can't be sure."*

obvious: robbery. Pyramids have been too prominent, too visible to elude the thieves who for centuries looted almost every tomb, temple, and memorial in Egypt. It seemed an archeologist's foolish dream to hope of finding one intact.

In 1951, however, that dream came true. Zakaria Goneim, a scholarly chief inspector of Egypt's Antiquities Department, discovered the buried remains of a previously unknown pyramid, one that had gone unnoticed by both archeologists and grave robbers.

Located at Saqqara, only six miles south of Giza, it had escaped detection because its builders had finished only the foundation, surrounding wall, and several stone courses of the pyramid itself—nothing too tall for the ever-drifting Sahara soon to cover. Goneim's early probings revealed an enormous, canyonlike cleft in the north side. It was the original entry, sloping downward as expected toward the anticipated funerary chamber.

Sand and rubble filled the entrance, rousing hopes that all below remained intact. Thoughts inevitably turned to Howard Carter's sensational discovery of only 30 years before—Tutankhamun's tomb. Would the Saqqara pyramid also yield a pharaoh's fortune?

Hopes soared when workers came up against one, then another stone wall barring the way. Surely no robbers would have bothered to reseal an entrance they had breached; these barricades must date to the pharaoh's interment some 4,500 years ago.

Beyond lay a warren of subterranean galleries and 132 storage chambers, all carved from solid rock. Goneim counted hundreds of stone, alabaster, and clay vessels, no doubt intended to hold supplies needed by the pharaoh in the afterworld. Five of them bore the unfamiliar name Sekhemkhet, meaning "powerful of body." Suddenly the pyramid was no longer anonymous; it belonged to King Sekhemkhet, a monarch who, like Tut, apparently had been forgotten by historians and vandals alike. Goneim was jubilant!

Other finds buoyed him even higher—beads of gold and carnelian, solid gold bracelets, and a gold cosmetic box expertly crafted in the shape of two hinged scallop shells. Here was proof that robbers had not ransacked the pyramid, for what thief willingly would have left such valuable and easily portable prizes? Now, to find the sepulcher and, perhaps, the king's remains. But the corridor led only to a dead end of roughhewn walls. Spirits plummeted—until Goneim spied the faint outline of a doorway, the third and best camouflaged barrier yet. Who could doubt that the burial chamber lay beyond, unopened and untouched since Sekhemkhet was laid to rest?

Anticipation gnawed at the men as they penetrated the ten-foot-thick barrier. Goneim, normally cautious, bubbled over. "At last," he later recalled, "when the final stone was removed, I crawled forward on my belly, electric torch in hand. We had broken through the blockage near the roof of a large vault. Below was black emptiness. Without further hesitation I plunged half-falling, half-scrambling, to the floor of the chamber." His assistant followed. "When we had picked ourselves up and a lamp was raised, a wonderful sight greeted us. In the middle of a rough-cut chamber lay a magnificent sarcophagus of pale, golden, translucent alabaster. We moved towards it. My first thought was, 'Is it intact?' "

Summit-bound climbers struggle up waist-high stones of Cheops's Great Pyramid. In the 13th century, Arabs stripped away its sheathing of smooth limestone to build Cairo's mosques. About 2.3 million blocks, some weighing

REBECCA COLLETTE

15 tons or more, make up this largest of all pyramids—originally 481 feet tall. No one knows exactly how the Egyptians quarried the stones and raised them into position, all without horses, iron tools, or the wheel. Mystery also shrouds this pyramid's creator. Cooney believes a granite sculpture (above) may portray the pharaoh Cheops.

riumph of the stonemason's art, the Great Pyramid reveals a superbly constructed yet mystifying interior. Cramped passages penetrate its bulk at odd angles—as shown in a diagram of 1843—leading to three different chambers, two of them unfinished. A granite coffer (bottom) occupies the uppermost room, which most scholars believe once held Cheops's mummy. Plain polished walls bear neither writing nor art and offer no clues to the chamber's use. A French expedition exploring the pyramid in 1798 marvels at the size of the Grand Gallery (right), marked by 28-foot ceilings. Now outfitted with stairs, it retains its imposing grandeur (opposite); experts find its purpose tantalizingly out of reach.

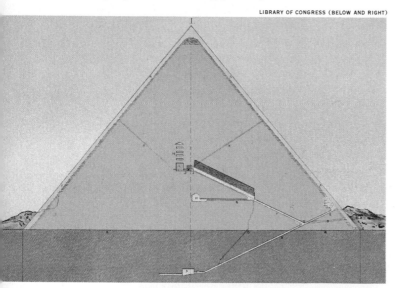

Indeed it was. Plaster still sealed its joints, and on top lay some decayed plant fragments arranged in a large V, apparently the remains of a wreath left by mourners. For nearly fifty centuries no eye had seen it, no light had touched it—until now. Goneim and his workers lost all control. "We danced round the sarcophagus and wept. We embraced each other. It was a very strange moment in that dark chamber, 130 feet beneath the surface of the desert."

Wisely, they did not open the sarcophagus at once. A month of careful preparations followed: clearing passages of debris, making detailed diagrams, and photographing the chamber. Antiquities Department officials arrived, expectant. The sarcophagus, unique in that it lacked a horizontal lid, had been skillfully cut from a single block of alabaster. A sliding panel at one end, plastered shut, provided access. Workers erected a scaffold and pulley to raise the 500-pound panel. Once more, thoughts of Howard Carter and King Tut darted through Goneim's mind. He signaled to begin.

Six men heaved on the pulley rope. Nearly two hours passed before the tightly sealed panel finally edged slowly upward. Goneim, aflutter with excitement, dropped to his knees to look inside.

The sarcophagus was empty.

All were stunned; no explanation seemed to fit. If the tomb had been robbed, why were its corridors mortared shut? Did tomb priests later discover the looted sarcophagus, reseal it and the tomb to appease the departed god-king? But it showed absolutely no signs of ever having held a body, wrappings, or coffin. Nor did it contain offerings or funerary trappings apart from the "wreath." This and the pyramid's obvious incompleteness convinced Goneim that no burial had ever taken place here. But then why all the storage chambers and jars, why the sealed sarcophagus and walled-up passages? If not to house the king's remains, what purpose had his pyramid served? To this day, Egyptologists cannot agree on an answer.

"You can argue in circles," says John Cooney. "There are just too many unknowns. We don't know what happened to Sekhemkhet and we probably never will find out."

Nor is his case an isolated one. The sands between Saqqara and Giza cloak another unfinished pyramid harboring a sealed yet vacant coffer. An extensively excavated step pyramid at El Kula, in southern Egypt, has never yielded a sarcophagus, a sepulcher, or even an entrance. American archeologist George Reisner did unearth gilt furniture and funerary equipment from the intact, nonpyramidal tomb of Cheops's mother, Queen Hetepheres, but her coffin held nothing.

Even Cheops's Great Pyramid shares in this sealed-but-empty syndrome, according to the man who seems to have been first to breach its upper levels, a ninth-century caliph named Abdullah al-Mamoun. He recorded his adventure in great detail, accurately describing the pyramid's complex interior with its system of massive blocking stones, all precisely fitted and wedged in place. Their intact condition led Mamoun to believe that no one had preceded him. Yet after he and his men penetrated these barriers and reached the sepulcher, they found only a lidless, empty, unmarked stone coffer.

Unsettling discoveries such as these—all but Mamoun's made in the last 80 years—have begun to pry a few scholars slightly away from the tomb theory. Says Cooney: "I used to assume the pyramids were burial places; it's still the easiest, most rational explanation. Yet the lack of evidence of burials bothers me; lately I've become a bit skeptical and have wondered if they really were tombs of kings."

Other evidence casts additional doubt. Why did Cheops's father, Snefru, who founded Egypt's Fourth Dynasty, erect at least two and quite possibly three huge pyramids, one of which contains two distinct entrances, each leading to its own tomblike room? The much later King Ammenemes III also has been credited with two pyramids. Although Cheops apparently built only one, it has three rooms—two unfinished—that may have been designed as crypts. Surely these pharaohs never intended to parcel out their remains in multiple vaults!

Nor did they intend the extra chambers and pyramids to entomb their queens or relatives, who were always interred in separate, lesser structures. No mortal, no matter how highborn, could share the sacred abode of a pharaoh.

Were the pyramids actually tombs? Herodotus of Greece thought so, but they were as ancient to him as he now is to us. Also, he was not a totally reliable reporter. In addition to recording Plato's Atlantis myth as fact, he wrote that the bowels of Cheops's pyramid sheltered an island surrounded by subterranean, Nile-fed canals—none of which ever existed.

What does exist is a marvel of precise engineering. Sir Flinders Petrie, a 19th-century archeologist who measured the Great Pyramid more accurately than any previous visitor, found that the lengths of its sides differed by a maximum of only eighty-eight thousandths of one percent! Its expertly laid exterior masonry, he declared, "is to be compared to the finest opticians' work on a scale of acres."

Such technical perfection grows even more remarkable in view of the pyramid's unique challenges. Haeny explains: "A cube, even a giant one, is fairly easy to build. You lay rows of stones one upon another, check that they are square, adjust for deviations, and so on. The pyramid is much more critical; its four sides slope smoothly up to a point—which, when you start, is only an imaginary one hundreds of feet above the desert. You can't sight on that point to check your work as you go up, because it doesn't exist. But if one face of your pyramid is just a little too steep, it will overshoot the others. You've no way to compensate except by changing the angle of slope midway—which would leave an undesirable bulge in the face. So once you lay the first course of stones, you're locked in."

Somehow the Egyptians succeeded with these elaborate construction projects. They also oriented the sides of most pyramids to cardinal points of the compass, often with astounding accuracy.

Despite such fine workmanship, the interiors of the major pyramids are curiously austere, and contrast with the floor-to-ceiling decorations lavished upon tombs of later queens and nobles. Cheops's granddaughter Mersyankh III, for example, merited a chapel full of sculptures, painted reliefs, and hieroglyphs near her crypt—

whereas Cheops's own coffer and pyramid walls were left bare. If other members of the royal family received such funerary recognition, why should Egypt's god-kings seek anonymity? "I suppose you could take the point of view that if Queen Elizabeth entered the room, she wouldn't give you a calling card," says Cooney. "But it has always puzzled me that all pyramids from the time of Djoser in the Third Dynasty until near the end of the Fifth Dynasty are completely, utterly blank."

Other nagging questions persist. Why did Cheops lace the interior of his immense pyramid with some 600 feet of passageways built to Lilliputian dimensions? Always less than four feet high, never equipped with stairs or even handrails, usually angled at a precise $26\frac{1}{2}$ degrees, these cramped and slippery corridors make extremely awkward thoroughfares. To walk here is to assume a crablike crouch and to scrabble slowly through the darkness, focusing on a distant square of light that is the tunnel's end. Heels repeatedly gouge into buttocks; vertebrae scrape the stone ceiling.

Yet Cheops's remains supposedly were transported along this same back-bruising path. One's mind balks, however, at the idea of pharaonic attendants, doubled over by the passage's subhuman proportions and encumbered with torches, slipping and sliding as they wrestle the king's heavy coffin, resting on a sledge, along the smooth, slanted floors. It's a vision that hardly holds with the dignified air of Egyptian funerary ritual.

It was also totally unnecessary. Pyramid architects easily could have raised ceilings and added stairways. Why make passages nearly impassable? Not to keep out robbers, for they surely would have had an easier time than heavy-laden attendants. Perhaps to keep something *in*? Curiously, the stone coffers of Cheops and his son Chephren are wider than the tunnel passages leading to them.

Tomb theorists speculate that narrow corridors were simply easier to seal shut. But the creators of earth's largest structures did not lack the stone or the manpower to build and then close up far larger passageways. In fact, at one point, the Great Pyramid's obsession with confinement gives way to awesome, uplifting proportions—the Grand Gallery. Suddenly you can stand! Eyes still nearsighted from the cramped passageways strain to make out ceiling stones 28 feet overhead. The corbeled walls gradually narrow as they rise, making the top seem even more distant.

It is a showpiece of the mason's art, grandly designed and expertly worked, without parallel in other pyramids. Blocks of limestone, some weighing 20 to 30 tons, have been cut, polished, and positioned so perfectly that their yards-long joints rarely exceed a hundredth of an inch! How did the Egyptians hand-smooth these massive stones and even harder chunks of granite to such exacting tolerances? More important, to what purpose?

"Why the Grand Gallery? I've no idea," says Edwards, and most of his colleagues agree. Its upper end leads to the so-called King's Chamber and the granite coffer. This room's construction is flawless, yet it comes as a strange anticlimax after the Gallery's spacious magnificence. It seems too small, its unmarked coffer too ignoble for a pharaoh's remains. Again, the doubt: Were pyramids truly tombs?

If so, they certainly were impractical ones. We know the ancients anticipated tomb robbery and believed their own welfare hinged upon the eternal preservation of the pharaoh's body. Surely they and their kings also realized that the best hope of success lay in secret burials, not in highly visible pyramids that would draw attention and the thieves they so feared.

Why, then, did they build pyramids?

One theory suggests they were cenotaphs—funeral memorials—possibly intended as earthly resting places for the king's soul or "for some religious or mystical purpose that we know nothing about," says Cooney. This would rationalize the pyramids' funeral implications with the consistent lack of mummies and tomb decorations. Cramped passages could be explained by the fact that souls need less space than flesh; coffers larger than corridors leading to them would prevent intruders from stealing the soul's earthly home.

Actual burial may have taken place in some secret, yet intact, cemetery—perhaps even in still-hidden chambers in the bedrock *beneath* pyramids. Robbers literally would have to move mountains to get to the mummies; each pharaoh's safety was assured for all time.

Dr. Kurt Mendelssohn, a prize-winning physicist also intrigued by the pyramids, believes these sentinels of the desert filled not only a religious need but also a political one—unification. In his book, *The Riddle of the Pyramids,* he notes that the four-century-long rule of Egypt's First and Second Dynasties left it less a country than a collection of widely scattered tribes that farmed, tended cattle, and fought almost constantly. The Nile's annual flood idled everyone for three months of the year, providing ideal opportunity, he suggests, to raid neighbors for livestock and women.

With the rise of Djoser's Third Dynasty, however, came peace—and the first stone pyramid. Was this coincidence? "We shall never know," writes Mendelssohn, "whether his foremost aim was the grandeur of the construction or the idea of employing troublesome villagers during the inundations." But pyramids were not just colossal make-work projects. Besides employing the idle, Mendelssohn theorizes, they also revolutionized society. "Tribal villagers were welded by common work into people with the consciousness of nationhood. It was probably for the first time they thought of themselves first and foremost as Egyptians."

Most Egyptologists readily reject Mendelssohn's concept, contending that a strong and unified Egypt was a prerequisite to building the first pyramid. Still, his theory neatly explains problems the tomb and cenotaph theories alone cannot, including the more-than-one-pyramid-per-pharaoh dilemma. If pyramids served primarily as the means to make a nation, several probably were under construction at any given time. This would ensure efficient use of Egypt's manpower. It also would reduce the mystery of Snefru's three pyramids to mere chance. Perhaps a predecessor began one or two of them but died during construction, leaving the glory of completion to Snefru.

Larger pyramids probably took 20 years or more to build, causing tomb theorists to wonder how a newly installed pharaoh could commit himself to making such a ponderous "tomb" when he had no idea whether he would live long enough to see the job through.

wice a pharaoh's bride, Cheops's aging daughter Hetepheres II oversees completion of her own daughter's tomb. Similarly lavish friezes and

inscriptions exalt nobles and their families in other tombs, but rarely grace a pyramid. This lack of funerary decoration adds to speculation that pharaohs built pyramids for reasons other than final resting-places, but raises another riddle: Where did the Egyptians bury all their kings?

The answer, according to Mendelssohn, is that he didn't. What mattered was not when or how many pyramids were completed, only that the work, and the new social order, continue. Interestingly, all three Giza pyramids contain hard Aswan granite, quarried nearly 600 miles to the south. With an excellent and oft-used supply of limestone right across the Nile from Giza, why did the pharaohs bother with the added difficulty and expense of granite? Were they motivated by a political yearning to bring their distant, southern frontier into the nationalistic fold?

It's only a theory, but an intriguing one. We know that some of Egypt's strongest kings—Djoser, Snefru, Cheops, Chephren—also were its greatest builders. The golden age of pyramids bloomed suddenly with Djoser's Third Dynasty and withered almost as suddenly toward the end of the Fourth, after little more than a century and a half. While the desire for pyramids endured through dozens of later reigns, the lust for massive proportions did not. Why? Was it simply that wealth and centralized authority declined? Or was it, as Mendelssohn reasons, that a century or more was sufficient time for pyramids to achieve their political goal? He writes that "the old tribal existence was largely forgotten. It was time to give up what had become an unnecessary and wasteful occupation. . . ."

Wasteful? Perhaps. But what an era! In that golden age Egyptians erected their seven grandest pyramids—one at Saqqara, another at Meidum, two at Dahshur, and three at Giza—containing altogether some 30 to 35 million tons of stone! How was this awesome mass quarried, moved, dressed, polished, and assembled in so little time by a people who lacked the wheel, iron tools, even horses?

Herodotus proposed that derrick-like levers hefted stones from one level to the next. Edwards believes that tens of thousands of laborers dragged the blocks up giant ramps that were enlarged as the pyramids grew. But the slope of these ramps had to be so gradual that they would have rivaled the size of the pyramids themselves!

On many fronts, we find the pyramids veiled in layer upon layer of contradiction and confusion. To study them is to stare at a shattered mirror: Countless fragments reflect only partial and distorted images, never a unified whole. Too few pieces fit together but, paradoxically, too many exist. Egypt has had so much history embalmed in its sands that, despite all the tomb robbers and souvenir seekers, an overwhelming quantity of artifacts still awaits discovery and analysis. Scholars know, for example, the location of thousands of tombs and monuments, but only a few sites have been excavated totally, with results published according to modern standards. Many areas never have been touched, such as part of Cheops's complex now covered by the town of Nazlet es Samman. Obviously, future archeologists will not lack for work. Might they one day find some written record explaining the pyramids in full?

Few think so. But who can tell? Within the last several years, some paleontologists have reversed the long-held view that dinosaurs were cold-blooded; and the recent theory of plate tectonics has unseated a centuries-old belief in a static earth. A similar revolution eventually may ignite Egyptology. Only one thing seems certain: As long as man's curiosity persists, so will the pyramids.

Glory of the pyramid age began to wane with the pharaoh Mycerinus, shown in this four-foot-high schist statue with one of his queens. A successor of Cheops, Mycerinus built the last and smallest pyramid in Giza's trio; his heir never built any. Succeeding dynasties returned to the pyramid form, but never equaled earlier ones in size or quality— perhaps for economic or political reasons.

NATIONAL GEOGRAPHIC
PHOTOGRAPHER VICTOR R. BOSWELL, JR.,
COURTESY MUSEUM OF FINE ARTS,
BOSTON

ver-changing hues of Giza's nightly "Sound and Light" show bathe the Sphinx and a pyramid, both built by Chephren, Cheops's successor. The

Sphinx's time-battered face probably once mirrored the king's features. Though scholars have dug through this artifact-strewn plateau for centuries, excavation continues. One day it may yield conclusive answers to the purpose and the meaning of Egypt's puzzling pyramids.

ANCIENT INDIA: CITIES LOST IN TIME

Far below the window of my plane, a slender strip of vibrant green slashed across a seemingly boundless sea of sand. Down the middle of this strip zigzagged a brown waterway—the life-giving Indus. As the plane descended, the strip of green resolved into a patchwork of fields, and the river spread wide and muddy.

Looking toward its west bank in Pakistan, the name of this land since its separation from India in 1947, I strained to see some sign of the lone mound that I was seeking. On the flat floodplain of the Indus it should stand out, I thought, this site of one of ancient India's first known cities.

Mohenjo-daro, "Mound of the Dead," people of Sind province have long called it. Not even legend suggests the name it went by when it was flourishing more than 4,000 years ago. No word, mural, monument, or tomb has revealed exactly who built it, how its influence spread over thousands of square miles, what caused its decline after some 500 years of prosperity, or why it was eventually abandoned and left to ruin.

At the mound, I knew that I would see the remains of fired-brick walls standing along an orderly arrangement of streets. "The oldest example yet known of systematic town planning," Sir Mortimer Wheeler called Mohenjo-daro in his 1966 account of its excavations.

Only a small portion of the city has been unearthed. The rest remains entombed in the silt and sand that stretches toward the Indus in the east.

Rising above the main body of the city is a smaller man-made area, dubbed the citadel by archeologists. It was constructed, early excavators reasoned, to raise the city's important buildings above the reach of river floods. It also created a stronghold higher than the main body of the city.

I had learned from archeologist Gregory L. Possehl that the mound of Mohenjo-daro—as well as a similar mound at the site of Harappa, about 400 miles to the northeast—had been mysterious oddities on the flat landscape for thousands of years. Local people apparently believed they were ancient graves.

"And they didn't leave the sites entirely alone," Dr. Possehl told me one rainy afternoon at the University of Pennsylvania in Philadelphia. Stacks of books about the Indus Valley culture and the Harappan people, as they are called, weighed down his office shelves; Dr. Possehl has devoted many years to pondering the mysteries obscuring their history.

"Some of the old bricks at Mohenjo-daro were used to build a Buddhist shrine in the second century A.D.," Dr. Possehl said. "At Harappa, very few of the ruins are still intact. In the late 1800's, the city's ancient bricks were carted away and used to build a railroad bed between Lahore and Multan.

"At the turn of the century, several archeologists were aware of the site, but no major excavations were undertaken until the 1920's. By then much of the site had been dismantled. But the digs did yield ancient artifacts, among them one-inch- to two-inch-square stone seals incised with pictures of animals, mostly bulls, and with what looked like a line of writing. Archeologists believed they were used to imprint wet clay that sealed packages of trade goods.

Overleaf: Bizarre animals, a horned deity, and a line of script cluster on the face of a steatite seal found in the ruins of Mohenjo-daro, one of ancient India's first cities. Carved more than 4,000 years ago, the tablet may have served as a personal insignia to mark the clay sealing on a package of trade goods. The horned, three-faced god looks surprisingly like the later Hindu deity Siva—perhaps a legacy passed on by the Harappan culture of Indian prehistory.

"At about the same time that Harappa was being excavated," Dr. Possehl continued, "an Indian archeologist began excavating the Buddhist shrine at Mohenjo-daro. To his surprise, he turned up some of the same curious seals. Spurred on by his discovery, he deepened and broadened his excavations and uncovered remains of far more ancient buildings. Here, apparently, was a second city belonging to the same culture as Harappa!

"These finds led Sir John Marshall, Director-General of Archaeology in India and the main force behind the excavation of both cities, to write in 1924 of the discovery of ancient India's first civilization. His description of the stone seals caught the attention of scholars studying the civilization of Sumer in Mesopotamia. They compared the Indus seals to similar objects now dated at about 2350 B.C. that were found in Mesopotamian ruins. They concluded that the two areas must have been in contact. Such conclusions meant that India had a highly developed culture by the third millennium B.C., and that it had been in contact with the so-called 'cradle of civilization.' But the nature of that contact is still debated today."

I asked Dr. Possehl about the physical evidence of interchange between the two regions. "Discoveries of Indus-like seals, beads, stone weights, and chess pieces have been made in Mesopotamia, along the Persian Gulf, and on the Iranian plateau."

Did the Harappans trade directly with the Sumerians, I wondered, or did goods move through a series of middlemen? Did the trade routes go overland across the Iranian plateau, or were there maritime connections between Indus Valley and Persian Gulf ports?

"Tantalizing clues come from Sumerian tablets that repeatedly

Living along the banks of the Indus River and its tributaries and along the coast of the Arabian Sea, the Harappans—named by archeologists for the site of one of their great cities—forged an advanced civilization based on agriculture, manufacture, and trade. In the third millennium B.C. they began to congregate in urban centers. Then, after some 500 years, the cities disintegrated. Scholars still ponder the reasons for the demise.

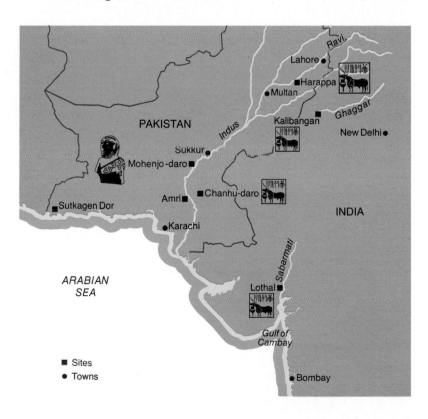

ARABIAN
SEA

PAKISTAN

INDIA

Ravi
Lahore
Harappa
Multan
Kalibangan
Ghaggar
New Delhi
Indus
Sukkur
Mohenjo-daro
Amri
Chanhu-daro
Sutkagen Dor
Karachi
Sabarmati
Lothal
Gulf of Cambay
Bombay

■ Sites
● Towns

Shadows lengthen across the crumbled ruins of the citadel at Mohenjo-daro, a sprawling city located near the west bank of the Indus River. A Buddhist shrine, built in the second century A.D. from the city's bricks, towers above the orderly arrangement of the citadel's structures—probably political and religious centers. Experts estimate

that some 40,000 people populated
Mohenjo-daro, living both on the citadel
and in the residential section of the
city. Archeologists can only guess at the
function of such artifacts as the clay
cones (right)—plumb bobs, writing
implements, or fishnet sinkers?

Craftsmen in a factory at Chanhu-daro, a Harappan town, produce steatite seals and gemstone beads. Protected from the fierce summer sun by an awning, workers saw the soft steatite into squares, then chisel images on their surfaces. A man inside the brick building shoves a tray of incised seals into a kiln. Scholars believe such organized production may have promoted trade; Harappan beads and seals have appeared in the ruins of ancient Mesopotamian cities.

mention maritime trade with three different places: Dilmun, Magan, and Meluhha. Many scholars believe one of these names, probably Meluhha, refers to the Indus Valley. Finds of Harappan artifacts on the Iranian plateau also indicate that there was overland contact, but we don't know if it was direct.

"If we could just decipher the writing on the Harappan seals," Dr. Possehl said, "we might find more complete answers to such questions. We've hoped that, through the seals, the Harappans could speak to us across the centuries. But so far, no decipherment and translation has been generally accepted."

Progress, however, has been made in discovering the extent of the culture. "More than 300 identified sites and 20 excavations," Dr. Possehl continued, "tell us that it dominated a triangle roughly a thousand miles long on each side, extending southwest from the Himalayas to the Arabian Sea, and then southeast along the coast from Sutkagen Dor to Lothal. Recent work in both Pakistan and India indicates that Harappan cities resulted from a long period of development. We now believe that the roots go back at least 7,000 years, to the earliest farming villages in the region. Contact with Mesopotamia may have been important commercially, but I don't think it was the major cause of ancient India's first urban revolution.

"The mystery that particularly intrigues me is what brought about the end of the cities. Mohenjo-daro and Harappa apparently were abandoned sometime after 2000 B.C. I don't think the traditional theories of invasion or ecological disaster provide satisfactory explanations. I believe that there must have been some crucially important part of their social organization that simply couldn't adapt to changing conditions. But," Dr. Possehl concluded, "no one knows exactly what happened."

In my travels, I would meet several archeologists, all of them struggling to piece together a picture of the Harappan culture from the relatively meager collection of artifacts. Only a few dozen seals show scenes with people. And of the pieces of sculpture that remain, just a handful have heads that reveal features of people.

But excavators have found many objects of terra-cotta: toy carts, pots, and figures of women, animals, and birds. And there are hundreds of tools and weapons made from stone, copper, and bronze.

Although much is still a puzzle about the Harappan civilization, the ruins of Mohenjo-daro reveal some things that archeologists can agree upon. Large residences and two-room rowhouses suggest a stratified society based on wealth. The planned street grid, a bath and drain in practically every house, and the same pottery traditions for some five centuries mean strong central organization.

"And for sure," Dr. Possehl had told me as we parted, "Mohenjo-daro is one of the best-preserved ancient city ruins in the world. Fired bricks have a better chance of enduring through long periods of time than sun-baked bricks."

I was now within minutes of walking among the extraordinary ruins of Mohenjo-daro. Below the plane, I could see ripening oranges growing in orchards next to golden wheat fields. Rows of cotton bearing bright white bolls reminded me that Indus Valley people produced cotton cloth centuries before anyone else in Asia, Africa, or Europe.

The landforms of today look much as archeologists think they did in Harappan times. Flashes of sunlight bounced from irrigation canals and ditches. "We've found no traces of ancient irrigation channels or neighboring farm villages, but the Harappans must have had them to feed a city of about 40,000," M. Ishtiaq Khan, Director of Archaeology for Pakistan, had told me earlier in Karachi.

Suddenly we were directly above the half-mile-wide Indus River. Gray-brown water streaked with white-sand islands flowed between whiter banks. In March, the Indus is calm and shallow. I could see boatmen moving their small crafts with poles. In midsummer, however, when snowmelt from the Himalayas surges downstream, the river becomes savage, "rushing onward like a bellowing bull," according to Hindu texts. Its floods can inundate a belt some 50 miles wide.

On the river's west side, in an area where only scrubby bushes grow on salty wasteland, a small hill jutted above the flatness. With a thrill of excitement, I glimpsed Mohenjo-daro's checkerboard of streets just seconds before the plane landed near the base of the hill.

Accompanying me was slim, mustachioed Muhammad Abdul Halim, an archeologist who had given up his fan-cooled office in Karachi to guide me through the hot, dusty ruins. The only ruin we could see from the runway was the Buddhist shrine.

"We believe its construction destroyed an important Harappan building," Halim said, "maybe a temple or a government center, since it's next to a large building that we think was possibly either the ruler's mansion or a college for priests. This structure is just across the street from a large pool—the Great Bath, it's called. Beside

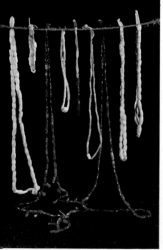

the bath is the granary, possibly a municipal storehouse for grain and other commodities that may have served as the economic bases of the culture. So right here, in a compact area, the Harappans seem to have had a power center."

The term "power center" contrasted sharply with the quiet rural scene before me—a barefoot, turbaned farmer urging along a donkey burdened with grass, a few old men smoking hookahs under a pipal tree. At the edge of the 35-foot-high hill, I noticed a man walking cautiously, balancing a large pan on his head. He stopped and poured dusty debris down the slope. I had the fleeting illusion of seeing a Harappan at work.

"He's getting rid of salt-corroded bricks," Halim informed me. "We have a crew replacing ruined bricks with new ones and also inserting waterproof slabs of concrete in the walls just above ground level. We hope these will block salty water seeping up from the ground." Irrigation and canal projects have raised the water table, and salts leached from the soil now lace the water. "Experts tell us the exposed parts of the ruins will crumble by the turn of the century if the water table isn't lowered and the bricks protected. Lowering the water table would also enable us to excavate the city's lowest levels, which are now flooded below ground."

In a burning March sun, we climbed flights of concrete steps mounting the citadel hill. Work, I realized, would be difficult here when summer heat rises to 110° F. or more.

Wilted by the sun and the climb, I escaped under the sparse shade of a lone acacia tree. There I took my first close look at the expanse of brick foundations and broken walls. I could easily identify the power center Halim had described. West of the Buddhist shrine, high walls flank a wide main street; a drain runs down its center.

Halim had strolled ahead and beckoned me toward the Great Bath. To get there, I walked down the main street. As I walked, I thought about the rulers of Mohenjo-daro who had probably crossed it in earlier days to go to the pool, which then was inside a building. Surely they went with ceremony, perhaps in a procession like the one pictured on a seal, with bearers carrying incense burners, a standard, and even a bull on a platform.

At the pool, Halim led me down a few steps to the rectangular brick floor eight feet below the surrounding court. Heat reflecting from the bricks mixed with the direct rays from above and seemed to double the temperature. Even so, a curious shiver overtook me. I looked about the walled bath and tried to imagine myself immersed in water, listening to chanting priests.

An early excavator, E. J. H. Mackay, suggested that religious rituals may have taken place in the pool, for a pool it surely must have been. Otherwise, why is there a drain and walls backed with bitumen waterproofing? Hindus still perform bathing rituals—stand waist-deep in water, immerse themselves, toss handfuls of water into the air, and pour water on their heads—in temple tanks as well as in sacred rivers and lakes.

"Most archeologists agree that the Great Bath was used in religious rituals," Halim said. "But when you feel heat such as this, you wonder if it was simply used as a swimming pool."

We continued on our tour of the ruins of the citadel, exploring the remains of buildings as long as 200 feet. Near the Great Bath, one structure had a long room divided into eight smaller chambers, each with a staircase. These apartments have been interpreted as private bathing rooms for priests.

At the south end of the citadel, a brick foundation supported a building some 90 feet square; its roof originally was held up by 20 columns. "We call it the Assembly Hall," Halim said. "But some think it might have been the bureaucracy's headquarters. If so, I wish we could find the written records that must have been kept there." He nodded toward nearby circles of earth in the brick paving. "For trees," he explained. I thought of Harappan figurines I had seen of monkeys and squirrels. I wondered if these creatures had scampered among the trees of Mohenjo-daro.

Soon we descended the citadel and walked across a wide depression to the residential part of Mohenjo-daro. Windowless walls as high as 20 feet shaded many lanes. Free-standing wells towered above the ruined buildings like round brick chimneys. "They gained height like the rest of the town as each new city layer was built on top of old debris," Halim told me.

We walked through spacious courtyards of multi-roomed mansions and through tiny enclosed yards of rowhouses; we peered into workshops; we inspected barrack-like chambers possibly used as storerooms or as quarters for servants. Finally, we came to a walled courtyard fronting a series of rooms. To me, it seemed like a motel. "Well, that's pretty close. It was probably a caravansary, a stopping place for caravans," was the response. "Bones of humped bulls, buffaloes, and asses have been found. Elephants were kept there, too."

Down every street, Halim pointed out narrow bricked drains. "Nearly every house, rich or poor, was connected to the city-wide sewer system," he said. No ancient city in Mesopotamia or Egypt, I reflected, had ever engineered such a system. But in Harappan cities and towns, the orderly grid of streets made it easy to lay out a drainage network.

Recent fieldwork by George Dales, a leading Harappan expert, and hydrological engineer Robert Raikes indicates that Mohenjo-daro was inundated by Indus waters several times. Excavations have revealed thick bands of silt in at least five building levels. That means water. The worst silt layers, each about two feet thick, seem to have occurred about 2000 and 1900 B.C. To escape this severe siltation, the people of Mohenjo-daro extended the walls of their houses vertically. Obviously they had dramatic fights from time to time with the forces of nature.

I pondered this fact the next day on my way from Mohenjo-daro to Harappa. After 500 years of prosperity, could recurring floods have destroyed the will of the people to live at Mohenjo-daro? I recalled a conversation with George Dales.

"Geological evidence points to events on a larger scale than mere river overflows," he had told me in his office at the University of

Wielding a mallet, a bead maker in India carefully chips a piece of carnelian using a method basically unchanged since Harappan times. After firing the rough pieces, which yields the deep red color, he will shape them into various forms for stringing. Modern necklaces (center) resemble ancient ones (bottom) found at the Harappan site of Lothal.

Cartload by cartload, families abandon Mohenjo-daro as conditions in the city worsen. Some experts theorize that heavy floods of the Indus

gradually brought about the decline; others believe that depleted land and resources eventually forced the Harappans to seek more fertile regions. Whatever the cause, the Harappan culture did not disappear, for it contributed to the foundations of India's later civilizations.

Pakistani workmen measure the windowless wall of a house in Mohenjo-daro. Harappans built many of their structures of fired bricks, which withstand the ravages of time better than sun-dried bricks. A rising water table bearing salts and corrosive minerals, however, threatens to destroy the ruins; workers now replace the lower courses of original bricks with waterproof slabs of concrete.

California, Berkeley. "Earthquakes and water. The Himalayan area has severe quakes regularly as the tectonic plate bearing the Indian subcontinent continues to plow farther into Asia.

"Indian paleontologist M. R. Sahni in the 1950's and Robert Raikes more recently found elevated silt deposits and rock faulting at two locations south of Mohenjo-daro. These represent ancient upheavals that could have blocked the Indus, forcing a ponding of its waters. That very thing happened southeast of Mohenjo-daro in 1819. Water backed up for about two thousand square miles, disrupting human habitation for years.

"We've now analyzed the silt between the layers at Mohenjo-daro. Five of the layers of silt resulted from still-water conditions, not from the flooding of a fast-moving river. Mohenjo-daro could have been isolated in a shallow lake for decades at a time. Probably during the final decades it was abandoned."

On the other hand, Harappa and other northern sites such as Kalibangan on the Ghaggar River show no significant silt layers leading to a decline in material prosperity. "We don't know how or precisely when Harappa was abandoned because the evidence was taken away when the site was dismantled for its bricks," Dr. Dales had told me.

For years the most popular theory for the decline of Harappa was that Aryan invaders from the north had overwhelmed it. But there is no evidence of Aryan presence until about 1200 B.C., long after the city was presumed abandoned. "Deteriorating conditions in Mohenjo-daro and southern towns such as Amri and Chanhu-daro," Dales explained, "probably disrupted the entire Indus Valley civilization. Harappa may have experienced problems because of the general breakdown of political and economic systems throughout the whole region."

So little remains of Harappa's citadel, and so little is exposed of the surrounding residential ruins, that the entire site can be toured in little more than an hour.

Only at the industrial and commercial area of the city could I sense even a vestige of the life of ancient Harappa. There I could imagine the rhythmic noise of wooden pestles grinding wheat on circular brick platforms and the cries of workers heaving grain into one of a dozen granaries.

In the museum at Harappa, Khan Muhammad, the site custodian, opened a showcase and laid into my palm a small Harappan trade seal made of steatite. I rubbed a finger over the delicate artistry of the incised carving of an animal. And what a peculiar creature it was. It had a bull's body, a long neck, and one graceful, protruding horn—perhaps the fabled unicorn.

Above the animal, I saw a line of symbols. To me they looked like a wheel, a long-toothed comb, two boxes on poles, a man with a bow and arrow, and two upside-down valentines. What could this message from the Harappans mean?

Many people, I knew, have tried to figure out such messages. Soviet scholars analyzing the script in the late 1960's concluded that the symbols stood for syllables and that the grammatical structure of the Harappan system was similar to that of the Dravidian languages found in southern India today.

Similar results were obtained by a group of Scandinavian experts working at about the same time. Using a computer in their analysis of the writing, they also concluded that the Indus script had a Dravidian character.

In New York, I'd listened to Professor Walter A. Fairservis, Jr., an American Indus scholar of long standing, explain his method for analyzing the script. He agrees that the language is early Dravidian. In addition, he believes that the script on the seals indicates the rank, title, and place of residence of the owner.

In India, Dr. S. R. Rao, superintending archeologist of the Bangalore district office of the Archaeological Survey, also has made a decipherment and translation of the seal writing. Dr. Rao is the excavator of Lothal, a southern outpost of the Harappans near the coast of the Gulf of Cambay. I arranged to meet him at nearby Ahmadabad and to drive to the isolated site.

During the hour-long jeep ride, I listened to Dr. Rao, a gentle and intense man of about 55 years, describe his work. Nearly all his life he has patiently picked away at the puzzles of the Harappans. "But I've never seen Mohenjo-daro," he said wistfully.

After 1947, the borders between India and Pakistan were closed. Dr. Rao was one of several Indian archeologists who began to search his country for Harappan sites. In the state of Gujarat, Dr. Rao found many. Combined with other sites in Rajasthan to the northeast, the known domain of the Harappans dramatically expanded.

Dr. Rao spent seven seasons excavating the most important of his sites, Lothal, which also means "Mound of the Dead." He believes that it was once a port on a river estuary, and that it was settled about 2450 B.C. by seafaring merchants of other Harappan cities. The Lothal excavation gave him the opportunity to investigate an undisturbed site. Artifacts were marked as they were found, and their positions in the site recorded.

"That enabled me to trace the evolution of the seal symbols and to look for the key to deciphering them," he told me.

"Dancing-girl," Mohenjo-daro's excavators called this more than four-inch-high bronze figurine, one of the most famous pieces of art from the Harappan culture. Only a necklace and bracelets adorn her.

Dr. Rao described how he sorted into some five dozen basic forms what at first seemed like hundreds of different seal symbols. He then traced the evolution of these forms from descriptive pictographs to simple stylized symbols and finally to abstract linear marks.

"I dared to imagine that these linear marks stood for individual speech sounds—an alphabet," he said. "Further analysis led me to believe that the linear marks represented an archaic form of Sanskrit, the language of the Aryans, and not Dravidian as many other Harappan scholars think.

"My translation of nearly all of the 3,000 seals found so far shows that they are titles and names," Dr. Rao continued. "The titles indicate a political hierarchy, I believe. The word divine is attached to some names. Other titles are Ruler of Rulers, Governor of Governors, and Great Protector. And still others are simply Protector, Governor, and Ruler."

Aristocratic mien marks the countenance of a steatite bust (right) found in the ruins of Mohenjo-daro. Archeologists speculate that the seven-inch-high statue may represent a person of political or religious importance. Called the Priest-King, the bust came from ruins in the city's residential section. Scholars think that Harappans used the Great Bath (below) for ritual bathing, a ceremony that continues today in the Hindu religion. A female figure (left), one of many found in the ruins, wears a fan-shaped headdress typical of such Harappan figurines.

NATIONAL MUSEUM OF PAKISTAN, KARACHI (ABOVE AND RIGHT)

Dr. Rao's theory, then, suggests that Aryans had trickled into ancient India about 2400 B.C.

He finds some support for his theory in the *Rig Veda*, sacred texts of the Aryans. "I believe the *Rig Veda* itself confirms that later Aryans recognized some resident people as Aryans like themselves," Dr. Rao contends.

"One ballad, for example, says the enemies they fought were 'some of ours.' Also, anthropologists who have examined skeletons from Harappan cemeteries have noted that the population then was an ethnic mix, much as it is today."

Under a sun even hotter than that of Mohenjo-daro, Dr. Rao and I slowly inspected the site of Lothal. At the east edge of the site, I saw a beautiful expanse of sparkling blue water in a brick-lined basin that covers about two acres. Although frequently dry, it fills with water following rainstorms.

"The dock," Dr. Rao has called this structure from the first, a judgment that has aroused controversy.

"I believe a channel connected the dock to a branch of the Sabarmati River flowing past the town," Dr. Rao said. "From there it was only a short distance to the sea. Gates and overflow channels controlled the water level in the basin. Merchant boats thus had a quiet pond for loading and unloading on a wharf that stretched the entire length of the basin—more than 800 feet."

American anthropologist Lawrence Leshnik suggests that the brick-lined cavity may have been used as a reservoir, perhaps as a source of drinking water and, more importantly, as a storage tank for irrigation water. Basins similar to the one at Lothal have been used for irrigation during much of India's recorded history and are still used in areas of southern India today.

The debate continues as to the purpose of the basin, but many scholars agree on the cause of Lothal's demise: floods. Total rebuild-

Silt-clogged and dry, a brick-lined basin stretches behind Lothal. It may have served the Harappans as a reservoir or as a dock for oceangoing boats. A clay model of such a boat (right) appeared in the ruins, perhaps indicating the town's role as a trading center. A seal also found there probably originated in a Persian Gulf port. It has creatures incised on the front (top left) and a boss on the back (bottom left). Stone weights, like the Harappan ones from Lothal (above), have turned up in Mesopotamian ruins.

ing followed a washout in 2200 B.C. A halfhearted reconstruction kept the town going after a flood in 1900 B.C., but a subsequent flood in 1600 B.C. brought abandonment.

"But at least until 1900 B.C.," Dr. Rao explained, "there is evidence, I believe, of trade with port towns on the Persian Gulf and in Mesopotamia. In the ruins of Lothal, we found pottery, a sculptured head, and gold beads—all of which I think are Mesopotamian. But the most important find was a small round seal like those used in Persian Gulf ports."

Many archeologists disagree with the interpretations Dr. Rao has made. But any answer to a question about the Harappans stirs up a new swarm of questions. Even experts who have devoted years of study to this civilization are divided on fundamental issues. And as Dr. Possehl had told me, "Without comprehensive texts and a means to decipher them, it will be difficult to have definitive answers."

Is it possible that the Harappans, so advanced in some ways, did not record anything—trading accounts, rules for their organized cities, even a personal letter? Or did they write only on unbaked clay or on some other perishable material that has disintegrated over the centuries? Or are the records somewhere waiting to be found?

I recalled a talk with Dr. M. Rafique Mughal, a handsome Pakistani archeologist I had met in Karachi.

"In the desert between Mohenjo-daro and Harappa," he said, "we've found two sand-covered sites as big as Harappa. There are also numerous smaller ones along the dry bed of a river, the course of which was diverted long ago by earthquakes. To excavate these sites would be very difficult, but I hope we can, someday. There's no telling what we might find there."

Perhaps buried in the dry desert sands of India and Pakistan will be clay tablets or other tangible evidence of the mysterious civilization of the Harappans.

olden glow of the setting sun washes the mile-
wide Indus River near Sukkur, a city 70 miles
upstream from Mohenjo-daro. A boatman poles

homeward in the evening stillness in a scene reminiscent of life thousands of years ago. Then, the Harappan culture dominated the Indus Valley, creating a sophisticated and innovative way of life that glowed brightly for a few centuries and then faded.

MEGALITHS: EUROPE'S SILENT STONES

by H. ROBERT MORRISON

photographed by ADAM WOOLFITT

Beads of dew clung to the grass, and a skein of fog hung over the River Boyne as I climbed a hill toward the ancient tomb of Newgrange in Ireland. Before me the huge mound containing the tomb rose like an apparition. In the chill, predawn light its facade of white quartz had lost its daytime glitter, enhancing the ghostly appearance. I glanced over my shoulder to the east and saw a thin pink glow beginning to outline the horizon. It was the week of the winter solstice, the shortest days of the year.

"Looks like it might be a good morning indeed," rolled the rich Irish brogue of caretaker Michael Smith. He opened the door to the tomb's entrance and turned on the lights inside. "You go on in," he said. "I'll let you know when the sun's about to come up."

Before me stretched a low passageway, a man-made tunnel in this man-made hill. Here and there were marks of flint tools where the ancient builders had shaped the stones lining the passage. Some 60 feet from the entrance I could stand upright inside a beehive-shaped chamber. Before me and on either side, smaller rooms were set into the walls. Each room held a saucerlike basin of stone about four feet across—presumably a receptacle for bones.

I had noticed designs carved into many of the stones of the passageway, but the interior of the chamber was lavishly decorated with them. Geometric patterns abounded in surprising variations—diamonds, triangles, concentric circles. One stone bore an incised triple spiral about a foot across. Its whirling grooves flowed into a dramatic unity as some lines snaked inward to form the spirals and others swept around the entire design. Clearly, I thought, this is the work of a master craftsman.

I had come to Newgrange on a journey in search of the megalith builders, enigmatic peoples of whom we know little except what we have learned from the remains of their monuments. Called megaliths for their huge stones, these monuments are found by the thousand throughout Ireland, Great Britain, and western Europe. The oldest date from about 4500 B.C., the most recent from about 3,000 years later. Their builders worked with tools of stone, wood, and bone. How did they organize great numbers of artists, craftsmen, and laborers for construction? And were they interested in geometry and astronomy, as their monuments seem to indicate? If so, how could they accumulate and pass on knowledge without a written language? Scholars have found no trace of one.

Suddenly a curtain of darkness dropped as the lights in the tomb went out. Michael's voice echoed up the corridor. "Get ready. The sun's just on the horizon."

I knew that the rays of the midwinter sun would shine directly into the tomb, but I was unprepared for what I saw. Down the passageway shot a shaft of light, glancing off the wall. It was a brilliant, fiery orange, totally unlike the gray gloom that I had left outside. As the sun rose, the beam reached farther into the tomb.

Its movement was unsteady; it seemed to stop for an instant, then probe on a few inches more. At last it touched the most distant wall of the chamber, pausing there for a moment, a thin red line across the stone. Then, just as it had entered, the light began its hesitant march back toward the entrance.

Overleaf: Monumental ruins dwarf visitors to Stonehenge, poised on England's Salisbury Plain. For centuries, such structures—called megaliths for their huge stones—have inspired myth and speculation. Today, despite thorough study by scholars, many questions persist about the megaliths and the people who built them. Recent surveys indicate that, during solstices, many monuments align with the rising or setting sun. Some experts theorize that ancient astronomers might have used them as instruments for the study of celestial events.

"I believe the builders planned this deliberately," archeologist Michael J. O'Kelly of University College in Cork told me later that morning. Professor O'Kelly, a slender man with sharp blue-gray eyes, directed the excavation and reconstruction of Newgrange. "I think the tomb was used in an annual ceremony. Now it's only speculation," he cautioned, "but I can imagine a yearly festival where the people gathered to honor the spirits of their departed leaders. As the sunlight shone into the tomb, perhaps the triumphs and failures of the year gone by were recited to the spirits of the revered dead, and their assistance requested for the year to come.

Thousands of megaliths —tombs such as Newgrange, ritual sites such as Avebury, and possible astronomical observatories such as Stonehenge and Callanish—stand scattered across Great Britain, Ireland, and western Europe. The oldest date from the Neolithic or New Stone Age, about 4500 B.C.; the most recent from the Bronze Age, some 3,000 years later.

103

"I feel sure," he concluded, "that Newgrange was not merely a tomb, but a major ceremonial center."

I recalled his words a month later as I drove through the gently rolling farmland of the Salisbury Plain in southern England on my first visit to Stonehenge. I entered the monument grounds on a bitterly cold and rainy day in January. Above me towered a circle of massive stones, some of them still capped with carefully shaped lintels. Within the circle were the remains of a horseshoe of smaller, darker stones, and above all loomed six huge single stones, two pairs of them also capped with lintels.

"Of course, what we see are just the remains of the last building phase of Stonehenge," red-bearded Mark Brisbane told me. A graduate student in archeology at the University of Southampton, Mark was my guide here. "It was begun about 2800 B.C. For the next thousand years or so, it underwent more or less continuous change—building, tearing down, and rebuilding."

Turning to a smaller stone about six feet high, Mark said, "This is one of the bluestones, so named for their bluish cast in dull light. About a century and a half after the first construction here, these bluestones were brought from the Preseli Mountains of Wales. By the combined land-and-water route archeologists believe the builders took, the distance is some 240 miles." What, I wondered, would have inspired such an effort of transportation?

Perhaps a clue can be found in one of the legends about Stonehenge. Writing in the 12th century, chronicler Geoffrey of Monmouth told of an ancient king of the Britons who wished to erect a monument in memory of some nobles. Merlin, a wise and powerful magician, advised the king to go to Ireland and bring back a sacred stone structure to be found there. An army made the journey and defeated the Irish, but the men were unable to move the stones. Merlin then constructed "wondrous engines," moved the stones across the water, and re-erected them with ease.

Although fanciful, this tale reflects the way archeologists believe the stones were moved. Professor Richard J. C. Atkinson, the excavator of Stonehenge in the 1950's, concludes that they were probably transported on rafts along the west coast of Britain and then up rivers on dugout canoes lashed together—not quite the "wondrous engines" of Merlin, but still a remarkable feat. If Geoffrey of Monmouth was recording an earlier tale, passed from generation to generation by word of mouth, the movement by water may have been an element of fact that remained through 35 centuries of retelling.

Originally there must have been at least 60 of the bluestones; today less than a third remain. The others have been broken up—for building stone, for road paving, even for souvenirs. At one time visitors could rent hammers in the nearby village of Amesbury to chip off bits of the stone as keepsakes. To me a very real part of the mystery of Stonehenge is that any of it remains at all.

Although archeologists can tell much about how Stonehenge was built, *why* it was built remained largely a matter of speculation until Gerald S. Hawkins, then professor of astronomy at Boston University and research associate at the Harvard College Observatory,

Shaft of light from a midwinter sunrise penetrates the stone-walled passage of a megalithic tomb at Newgrange, Ireland. Built some 5,000 years ago, the tomb has a special opening above the entrance that allows the rays to reach the farthest extent of the chamber on the shortest day of the year. Despite changes in the earth's axis of rotation, the phenomenon still happens today.

MIKE BUNN

105

Flickering oil lamps and the dawning sun light the tomb at Newgrange on the winter solstice. Worshipful attendants, protected from the cold by garments of wool and leather, bow low before presenting offerings of meat and produce during a ceremony to honor their ancestors.

began a study of Stonehenge in 1960. With the help of a computer, he calculated the positions of the sun and moon over Stonehenge during its period of construction. He then concluded that the monument was an observatory for studying cycles of the sun and moon.

At first, archeologists greeted Dr. Hawkins's findings with skepticism. Reactions ranged from sober discussions of mathematical probabilities to instant dismissal because the builders of Stonehenge "just weren't that smart." But as the debate ebbed, more and more archeologists began to accept many of Dr. Hawkins's major findings.

As we walked about, Mark showed me a few of the ways the ancient astronomers could have used Stonehenge. "The midsummer sunrise over the Heel Stone is the best-known alignment," he pointed out, "but there are many others. For example, if you stand here and sight through the space between those large outer stones, you're looking where the full moon will rise at its southernmost extreme."

Until the early 1970's, most archeologists considered Stonehenge and other megaliths a result of the gradual westward spread of civilization from its Middle Eastern cradle. Daggers carved on Stonehenge rocks, for instance, are similar to daggers found in the ruins of Mycenae in southern Greece. And radiocarbon dates for wood and other organic material found at Stonehenge and similar monuments showed them to be built after the Mycenaean civilization.

This comfortable scenario was shaken after researchers found that some bristlecone pines growing in California's White Mountains had lived for more than 3,000 years. By comparing samples, first from living trees and then from trees long dead, scientists could count the annual growth rings and tell the age of the wood back for thousands of years. Here was a standard for dating wood samples. Comparisons quickly showed that many established dates—including those of the megaliths—were too recent.

"But doesn't that mean the accepted dates for the Mycenaean civilization were also off?" I asked Professor Colin Renfrew when I visited him at the University of Southampton, England. Professor Renfrew was one of the first archeologists to recognize the implications of what has been called the "revolution in radiocarbon dating."

"No, it doesn't," he replied. "In western Europe, archeologists relied on radiocarbon dating because of the lack of written records. In the study of civilizations like the Mycenaean, the ages of sites were often determined with precision by written records found there.

"What this means for the megaliths," he continued, "is that they were being built before the rise of the civilizations we had thought to be their source. It now appears that the inhabitants of western Europe were the continent's first architects and builders in stone."

The following days I spent visiting other ancient sites nearby, for Stonehenge is merely the most prominent of a cluster of megalithic tombs, stone circles, and circular earthworks known as henges.

To me the most remarkable of all is Avebury. As Mark and I drove toward it, we followed a double line of upright stones marching for almost a mile beside the road. Then a ring-shaped embankment appeared before us. Its grassy slopes rose above our car as we drove through a gap in the bank and entered the village now located within the ring. We climbed to the top of the great earthen circle, and

Slanting capstone 13 feet long tops the portal dolmen of Poulnabrone, a tomb in County Clare, Ireland. It rises above the Burren, a convoluted plateau of weathered limestone. Some 150 similar tombs dot the countryside of Ireland. Experts believe that ancient people buried revered dead in such places, although why they moved and erected the large stones—some weighing as much as a hundred tons— remains a mystery.

I stood awestruck by the sheer size of it. "You really can't compare its appearance now," Mark reminded me, "with the way it once looked. The ditch that surrounds the ring provided material for the mound, and originally it was a lot deeper. About 15 feet of earth has washed into it over the years. When first built, the top of the mound was at least 50 feet above the bottom of the ditch. The circumference of the bank is about four-fifths of a mile, and the area inside is more than 28 acres."

"When was it built?" I asked.

"Before 2000 B.C.," Mark replied. "It was complete when the bluestones were taken to Stonehenge."

As we looked down within the earthen circle, Mark pointed out other features. "At one time about 98 huge stones lined the inside of the circle. The heaviest of them weighed more than 60 tons, and the tallest was at least 19 feet high."

Within the great circle were erected two other rings of standing stones, each ring more than 300 feet across. Today, few of the stones remain. Many were broken up in medieval times, when the villagers believed they might have been set up by the Devil. For all its dramatic size, I learned, Avebury is still a puzzle. About all that archeologists agree on is that it was an important religious center.

After visiting Stonehenge, Avebury, and several other sites nearby, I wanted to see a place where the people of that long-ago time had actually lived, not just come for ceremonies or burials. I flew north to the Orkney Islands off the north coast of Scotland.

The islands were spread with a mantle of new grass and dotted with brilliant wild flowers. Not until I had driven several miles did I notice the absence of trees. Then I realized that many of the fields were bounded by stone fences—regularly shaped slabs piled neatly layer upon layer.

My first destination was Skara Brae, a Neolithic settlement along the Bay of Skaill on the west coast of Orkney. Ronald Miller, a retired professor of geography from the University of Glasgow, had shown me about on an earlier visit, and I reflected on what I had learned from him as I walked toward low green mounds. "This settlement is unique, not only because it is one of the few living sites we have found from the Neolithic period, but also because it is so well preserved. Due to the scarcity of wood, the buildings were made of stone, and so was much of the furniture in them. For undetermined reasons, the village was abandoned in haste, and the inhabitants left behind many of their tools and ornaments. Windblown sand quickly covered the settlement, sealing it for the future. And so Skara Brae has enabled archeologists to compile a complete picture of everyday life there nearly 5,000 years ago."

That was easy to believe as I looked into one of the dwellings. Along one wall three rectangular slabs of stone stood on edge. When filled with heather or furs, they formed a bed. Other slabs made a cupboard complete with shelves. In the center was a hearth, and near it lay a stone mortar for grinding grain. Set into the floor was a tank of slate, its corners chinked with clay to make it watertight.

Passageways walled with stone, barely wide enough for one

person, wound among these subterranean dwellings. The walls held back the midden—garbage and refuse—mounded all around the dwellings. In summer, the stench must have hung like a cloud about the village. But in winter, the refuse helped shelter the dwellings from wind and storm.

From bones found in the midden, we know that these people raised cattle and sheep for food. They liked beads and pendants, fashioning them from shell, bone, and the ivory of walruses and narwhals. Traces of red, yellow, and blue pigments, probably used as cosmetics, were found in small stone cups.

Were these people similar to those who created the megalithic monuments? Perhaps. But this tiny community of some half-dozen families was isolated, almost entirely on its own. We have no assurance, therefore, that it typifies the communities of the megalith builders. As I left Skara Brae, the mystery remained with me.

Orkney is rich in megalithic remains, among them Maeshowe, perhaps the finest example of an ancient tomb in Great Britain. As I stooped at the 4$\frac{1}{2}$-foot-high doorway, I felt as though I were entering a long stone box. For the first eight feet, the walls of the passage were layers of stones; but for the remaining 16$\frac{1}{2}$ feet its walls and roof were formed of huge slabs. As I stood up in the tomb and looked about, I was struck by the beauty of its elegant yet simple architecture. Large pieces of sandstone were laid in true and level courses, many of them single stones extending the entire length of the wall. A chamber about five feet across and three feet high was set into each wall except the one with the passage doorway. Each chamber was roofed with a single stone slab. (Continued on page 118)

Earthen rampart 1,380 feet in diameter rings the village of Avebury, England. Within the 30-foot-high bank stand the remnants of three circles of upright stones, the largest of them more than 19 feet tall. The complex probably served as a religious or ritual center, but no one knows the significance of its circular shape.

Brisk North Atlantic wind whips visitors at the Neolithic settlement of Skara Brae in the Orkney Islands off Scotland. Soon after villagers abandoned these dwellings, drifting sand covered the site, preserving a unique record of everyday life here some 5,000 years ago. Within the huts stand furnishings of stone. At right, a cabinet against the far wall has four compartments; slabs of rock near the other walls form beds, once probably filled with springy heather or furs; a rectangular hearth occupies the center of the room. Crafted from jadeite, a ceremonial ax (far right), discovered near Carnac, France, dates from the same period. Similar ones found throughout western Europe give evidence of wide-ranging trade among Neolithic peoples.

Like an army in formation, rank upon rank of stones march toward houses in the village of le Menec, near Carnac. Some 2,500 of the towering rocks form arrow-straight rows that extend for miles across the landscape of Brittany (below). The first scholar to survey these alignments with detailed precision, Professor Alexander Thom of Scotland, suggested in 1971 that they served as computing grids—complex graphs used for solving mathematical problems associated with astronomy. Thom contends that ancient astronomers used these stones in conjunction with other

FRENCH GOVERNMENT TOURIST OFFICE

nearby monuments to keep track of the movements of the moon. Not all scholars agree. The debates over his theories show few signs of ceasing, and the purpose of these stone rows remains unknown.

115

Whorled lines, expertly incised by artists some 5,000 years ago, blanket stones supporting the roof of a tomb on the island of Gavrinis off Brittany. This motif of swirling lines appears in megalithic art throughout western Europe, although experts disagree on what it represents. A stone from a grave near Carnac (top, right) suggests a female figure to some; until the late 1950's, scholars referred to it as a cuttlefish. Some authorities have speculated that it may provide evidence of a cult honoring a powerful goddess. Below it, two small stone idols discovered in Spain represent this goddess to some researchers; others note an owl-like

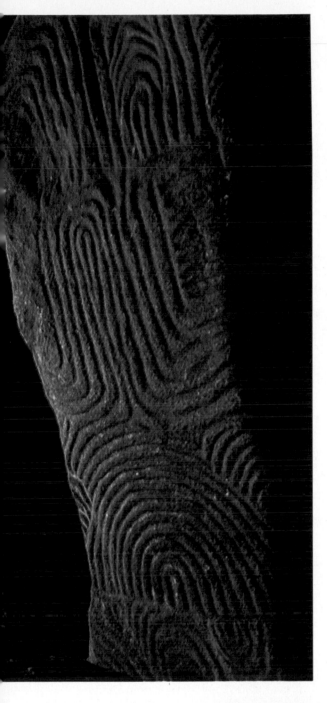

appearance. A chiseled
stone ball, one of many
found in Scotland,
measures three inches
in diameter. Its use
unknown, the ball bears
patterns similar to
those on the megaliths.

"The largest of the stones here," Professor Miller had told me, "weighs more than three tons. Even today, some of the joints are fitted so closely that you cannot insert a knife blade into them."

Upon leaving the tomb, I paused for a moment to look across the fields toward the lochs of Harray and Stenness. On a neck of land separating their sparkling waters, I could just make out my next stopping place, the mystical Ring of Brogar.

Only 27 of an estimated 60 stones remain here, set inside a circular ditch 370 feet in diameter. The flat sides of the stones face inward, and the tallest of them rises 15 feet above the ground.

Why was it built? One man has advanced a remarkable theory to explain its existence.

In the 1930's Alexander Thom, a Scottish professor of engineering at Oxford University, began making careful surveys of stone circles throughout the British Isles. His chartings generally were the most accurate yet made—indeed, for many sites, the only accurate ones. He surveyed the Ring of Brogar in 1971 and again the following year, and soon reached the startling conclusion that it was a sophisticated lunar observatory.

An ancient astronomer standing at the center of the ring, Professor Thom points out, could see four natural landmarks on the horizon. Each of them coincided with where the moon rose or set on one of the important dates of a cycle of 18.6 years. The landmarks—or "foresights"—are accurately indicated by lines of mounds or cairns lying near the ring and pointing directly at them. By sighting down these lines, the astronomer could study small irregularities in the moon's movements caused by the pull of the sun's gravity. This knowledge would have helped in the prediction of eclipses.

The easiest foresight to see today is the slope of a high cliff five miles to the southwest. The moon appears to slide down this slope as it sets on one of the important dates. By preserving this kind of information generation after generation, the astronomers at the Ring of Brogar would have discovered predictable cycles in the moon's seemingly erratic course. In his report on Brogar Professor Thom wrote, ". . . when we think of the difficulties which had to be overcome, we wonder how long it took to establish this observatory and how much effort was involved."

Besides the Ring of Brogar, Professor Thom visited hundreds of other megalithic sites. From his meticulous research, based on thousands of measurements, he drew three major conclusions: First, that many sites were aligned with prominent features on the horizon for the purpose of making precise observations of the movements of the sun and the moon. Second, that many of the rings were not strictly circular, but variations constructed through the use of sophisticated geometry. And third, that in Britain and Brittany the builders of the stone circles and rows had used a common unit of measurement exactly 2.72 feet long, which he called the megalithic yard.

His scientific papers in the 1960's and early 1970's provoked a storm of argument among archeologists, astronomers, and mathematicians—a storm that still rages. Although even the most conservative scholars generally acknowledge the accuracy of Thom's data, many disagree with his conclusions. The fact that mathematicians today can use the stones for observations, they contend, doesn't prove that the builders of the circles did. And because we can reproduce their shapes through the manipulation of geometry doesn't mean that the builders did so thousands of years ago. And finally, they say, Thom's megalithic yard implies communication and close coordination among widely separated groups that shared common values. Only a few scholars believe the evidence supports that viewpoint.

Professor Thom was inspired to begin his studies in 1934 when he noticed a group of megaliths while sailing his yacht off the Isle of Lewis in the Outer Hebrides. I decided to visit the Standing Stones of Callanish to gain an insight into Thom's theories.

My guides at Callanish were Margaret and Gerald Ponting,

Circling a bonfire, dancers in County Cavan, Ireland, mark Midsummer's Eve with a ritual that may have had its beginnings in the Stone Age. Other customs, many scholars believe, share roots as old. Girls in Derbyshire, England, spray flower petals and greenery covering a well. This annual well-dressing ceremony, based in ancient tradition, celebrates spring and the gift of water. In a field near the village of Abbots Bromley in Staffordshire, horn dancers carry reindeer antlers as they perform one of the oldest dances in Europe. It may have begun thousands of years ago as a ritual to honor the reindeer and to ensure a good hunt.

schoolteachers and amateur archeologists who have made extensive studies of the site. From a nearby rocky outcrop I could see the monument. Rows of stones formed a gigantic cross more than 400 feet long. In the center, within a ring of 13 tall stones, a single huge megalith towered nearly 16 feet above the remains of a small grave.

When Alexander Thom stood on this same rocky outcrop that evening in 1934, he noticed that the North Star shone directly in line with the north-south row of stones. "Later surveys established that this row was laid out with an accuracy of a tenth of one degree," Margaret told me.

"Both Thom and Hawkins have proposed a number of ways ancient scientists could have used Callanish for studying the movements of the sun and moon," Gerald added. "For example, an astronomer could have stood at the end of one of the short arms of the cross. By sighting along that row, he would see where the sun rose at the equinoxes, the two days of the year when day and night are the same length. Many other alignments involve one or more stone circles. We have identified more than a dozen such sites within a few miles of here."

After my visit to Callanish, I had seen in Britain and Ireland a sampling of what one 19th-century writer called "rude stone monuments." However, I had yet to see any on the continent of Europe. Near Carnac, France, I found a concentration of ancient graves and standing stones.

I began my exploration there at the most widely known of the megalithic sites—the great avenues of stones. Some 2,500 of them jut from the ground in parallel rows miles long, looking like so many soldiers in columns. I hiked among these stones on a summer afternoon, the air filled with the murmur of bees collecting nectar from bright yellow flowers. I felt a sense of both wonder and frustration: wonder at the motives that inspired men to such effort, and frustration at my inability to comprehend the meaning of that effort.

The following day I visited a site that Professor Thom believes holds a key to part of that mystery. On the Locmariaquer Peninsula a few miles east of Carnac lie four great stones, the broken pieces of the Grand Menhir Brisé. When standing, the huge pillar would have reached between 65 and 70 feet high.

After weeks of measuring and surveying there, and subsequent months of study back in Scotland, Professor Thom suggested that the Grand Menhir Brisé could have served as a universal foresight to be used for observing the moon's movements from certain locations in the surrounding countryside. And he shows that the alignments at Carnac might have been a computing grid, a kind of graph in stone to assist in working out the complex mathematics involved in the calculations. While much of the evidence seems to support Thom's theory, scholars are still debating his conclusions.

Just a few yards from the fallen stone, I entered a grave called La Table des Marchands, the table of the merchants. Here a capstone 21 feet long, 12 feet wide, and 6 feet thick rests on a few standing stones. At the end of the chamber, mysterious symbols cover one of these upright stones.

The face of the nine-foot-high megalith has been chipped away, leaving raised lines that somewhat resemble upside-down hockey sticks. Another raised line borders the stone, with curved lines running outward from it like a fringe. The roughly triangular shape of the stone repeats a design that appears in many such graves. Archeologists have seen it as a shield, a cooking pot, the sail of a ship, or a stylized mother goddess. They have suggested that the hockey sticks may represent ax handles, rows of grain, streamers on a ship's sail, or shepherds' crooks denoting authority.

I found another explanation when I talked with Professor P. R. Giot in his book-lined office at the University of Rennes. Professor Giot is the director of research at the Laboratory of Prehistoric Anthropology there, and he knows more about the prehistory of Brittany than any other man in France.

Our discussion turned to megalithic art, and I mentioned that to me the hockey sticks looked like a field of grain. "Wait here a moment, and let me show you something," he said, his eyes twinkling. He returned with a scientific paper and handed it across the desk to me. "That photograph shows a Stone Age sickle found in river sediment. Now, what does that remind you of?"

I studied the photograph. A sharpened stone blade was wedged into the short end of an L-shaped wooden handle. I turned the photograph sideways and immediately saw the resemblance. The sickle looked exactly like the hockey sticks. Perhaps, I thought, a bit of the mystery was solved.

I returned to Stonehenge on the evening of the summer solstice. I thought that perhaps watching the sunrise there would help me in some way to feel what a visitor of 4,000 years ago might have experienced. I was not alone in my thoughts. Thousands of other people thronged to Stonehenge that night—some to party, some to pray, and some, like me, to try to discover part of the legacy of the megalith builders.

About 4 a.m. a police officer opened the gate to the monument grounds. I presented my pass and walked in with a crowd of others. In the darkness, I wandered among the ominously looming stones. They felt cold to the touch—but to me the chill was more than just that of one night. It seemed that I could sense the cold of a million nights stored up in these silent stones.

After several long hours, the eastern sky began to lighten. White-robed Druids, a modern mystical group that claims Stonehenge as a ceremonial site, performed a slow-paced ritual in the center of the megalith. The sun slowly rose, but a low bank of clouds hid its face; only a diffuse golden glow marked its passage. Although I was disappointed, I still felt a surging sense of wonder and mystery on that cold, cloudy morning.

During the course of many months, I had sought the megalith builders among their most magnificent creations; I had searched for the meaning of their grand structures; and I had tried to imagine what the builders' lives might have been like. Yet here, at the end of my travels, their purpose remained as elusive to me as the face of the sun on that midsummer morning.

tanding Stones of Callanish jut before a westering
sun as summer gloaming lingers on the Isle of
Lewis off Scotland. Once called a temple but also

considered an astronomical observatory, the structure symbolizes the mystery of Europe's silent stones. Forty centuries ago its builders died, leaving behind an enduring monument—and a source of wonder and puzzlement to those who seek to understand the enigma of the megaliths.

MINOANS: A JOYOUS PEOPLE VANISHES IN MYTH

by CHRISTINE K. ECKSTROM

photographed by GORDON W. GAHAN

The Gorge of the Dead splits the earth as if struck by the ax of a god. From its mouth a small, fertile valley widens toward the eastern shore of the island of Crete. High on the chasm's walls, black caves gape with the vacant stare of skulls. Once people climbed to the caves to bury their dead.

These people were considered ancient by the people we call ancient Greeks. And in a time that falls in the half-light of human memory, they created a civilization whose achievements still dazzle the world four thousand years later. The Bible names their land Caphtor. Ancient Egyptians called them Keftiu. Homer says their king was Minos: We know them now as Minoans. No one is certain where their forebears came from or when they first touched the shores of Crete. But between 3000 and 1450 B.C., Minoan power and culture rose to full splendor, and the first civilization in Europe was born.

Far greater mysteries than the question of their origins surround the Minoans. For despite more than 75 years of study, no one knows what language they spoke or what message lies in their written words. Minoan civilization stands before us like "a picture book without text," as one scholar has noted. We do not know who ruled their lands—kings or queens, priests or priestesses—or why maidens and youths risked their lives to vault over the horns of charging bulls. Some scholars have speculated that the Minoan world embraced Atlantis, for, like that sparkling island civilization imagined by Plato, the Minoans disappeared and soon were forgotten.

Minoan Crete must have seemed a fairyland to travelers in 1500 B.C. Magnificent palaces, luxurious villas, and bustling towns sprinkled the mountainous countryside. From its harbors mighty fleets set sail for the far frontiers of the world it knew—Egypt, the Near East, and Greece—laden with timber, pottery, and agricultural goods. Across the Aegean and eastern Mediterranean seas the sailing ships coursed, and they returned to Crete bearing treasures of gold, ivory, and precious stones.

From the hands of Minoan craftsmen and artists came masterpieces of exquisite beauty: delicate carvings on tiny stones and gems; finely wrought jewels of gold; eggshell-thin pottery glowing with wild, free designs; glorious frescoes of leaping dolphins, dancing women, fantastic landscapes. All these bespeak the refined sensibilities of the Minoans. Through their arts they reveal themselves as a people exuberant with new ideas and the joy of life.

Then—silence.

The Keftiu came no more to the shores of Egypt. They survived in colorful frescoes at Thebes as a phrase in Egyptian history.

Slowly, slowly, the soil and the centuries encroached on the palaces of Crete, and what happened in the days of King Minos dimmed in the memory of Aegean people. But as the centuries passed, they gathered around their hearths at night to hear the melodic words of bards singing stories of their ancestors who lived in a glorious time.

In the eighth century B.C., the Greek poet Homer wove tales from the lips of these bards into two epic poems, the *Iliad* and the *Odyssey*. Greece had emerged from a dark age, and two centuries after Homer the Classical era began. The Greeks of that time believed that Homer's words held their history. More than two thousand years

Overleaf: Prince of a peaceful land, a Minoan youth strides with grace and elegance in a reconstructed stucco relief from the Palace of Minos at Knossos. Between 3000 and 1450 B.C., the Minoan civilization flourished on the Mediterranean island of Crete—then faded away. Their origins unclear, their language unknown, their fate obscure, the Minoans still puzzle archeologists who seek to unravel the mysteries that cloak the founders of Europe's first great civilization.

ARCHAEOLOGICAL MUSEUM OF IRAKLION, CRETE (OVERLEAF)

after the Classical Greeks, 19th-century scholars read Homer's description of a wondrous place: "Out in the dark blue sea there lies a land called Crete, a rich and lovely land, washed by the waves on every side, densely peopled and boasting ninety cities. . . . One of the ninety towns is a great city called Cnossus, and there, for nine years, King Minos ruled and enjoyed the friendship of almighty Zeus. . . ." They smiled at Homer as a weaver of dreams.

Then, in 1900, an Englishman named Arthur Evans startled the world. Evans was a man alive with curiosity. He was curious about the peculiar symbols on tiny stones sold by antiquities dealers in Athens. As the Keeper of Oxford University's Ashmolean Museum, he had long been fascinated by ancient scripts; the strange markings looked like a kind of writing. Where had they come from? "Crete," was the answer.

Evans thought hard about Crete, for he was lured by places where traditions were rich and history pervasive, places where ghosts walked. Crete was such a land, and he explored it in 1894.

Zeus, a powerful god, was born high in a mountain cave on the island. His son Minos ruled Crete and made her mistress of the seas. From Poseidon, god of the sea, Minos received a beautiful bull, and his wife, Pasiphae, fell in love with the creature and bore the Minotaur—half-man, half-bull. Deep inside his palace at Knossos, in the heart of a dark labyrinth, Minos kept the hulking Minotaur.

After years of study and reflection on such legends, Evans returned to Crete. Iron-willed and energetic, he was determined to find more engraved stones and to learn of the people who once fashioned the script. Perhaps, he thought, some truth lay hidden in the myths of Crete. Just inland from the modern port of Iraklion stood a mound called Kephala, the legendary site of Knossos. Evans was a wealthy man; he bought Kephala. And in March 1900, he sank his spade into the mound and began to unearth a magnificent palace.

Seaside sentinels, four ancient palaces rise near the shores of Crete, where harbors once sheltered mighty Minoan fleets. Masters of the eastern Mediterranean, the Minoans traded at ports from Egypt to Greece and influenced places like Thera, 70 miles to the north. A small volcanic island, Thera erupted about 1500 B.C. in a series of cataclysmic explosions that may have upset the Minoan world.

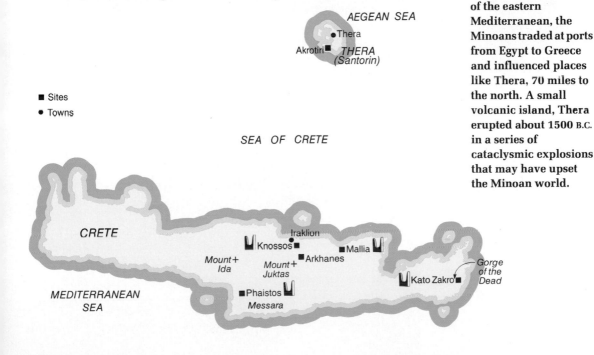

AEGEAN SEA

●Thera

Akrotiri■ *THERA*
(Santorin)

■ Sites
● Towns

SEA OF CRETE

CRETE

Iraklion
Knossos■
■Mallia
Mount+ Ida
Mount+ Juktas
■Arkhanes
Kato Zakro■
Gorge of the Dead

MEDITERRANEAN SEA

■Phaistos
Messara

Myth springs to life at the Palace of Minos, once the shining center of Minoan Crete. The palace today reflects the labors of archeologist Arthur Evans, who began excavations at the turn of the century and worked for more than 25 years to reconstruct the crumbled complex. Its maze of rooms and corridors lends a flicker of truth to the legend of the labyrinth where King Minos hid the horrible Minotaur—half-man, half-bull. The bull-leaping spectacle, depicted in a fresco (opposite, lower)

ARCHAEOLOGICAL MUSEUM OF IRAKLION, CRETE (LEFT)

from Knossos, may show a link to the myth. Stylized horns on the palace wall (right) and a bull's-head rhyton, a ritual vessel (above), suggest the Minoans revered the bull—symbol of fertility and power.

EKDOTIKE ATHENON S.A., ARCHAEOLOGICAL MUSEUM OF IRAKLION, CRETE

Like all archeological finds, the palace at Knossos posed more mysteries than its discovery solved. Here, where Evans had found a forgotten civilization, I began my quest to understand the haunting questions that still surround the Minoans.

On a bright April day, I climbed a hill above Knossos and turned to look down on the ruins that Evans called the Palace of Minos. Its buff buildings spread like honey over the mound of Kephala, cupped in low, rolling hills. To the southwest rose the sacred peak of Mount Juktas, where Zeus is said to have died each year after the harvest. Through a gap in the hills that fall to Crete's north coast, the blue of the Aegean waters met the blue of the sky.

Inside the palace, the colossal labors of Arthur Evans have breathed life into a masterpiece of ancient architecture. Evans devoted his fortune and more than 25 years of his life to reconstructing the Palace of Minos and to resurrecting the spirit of its creators. His efforts have been both praised and scorned, but as respected archeologist J. D. S. Pendlebury wrote, "Without restoration the Palace would be a meaningless heap of ruins. . . ."

As I wandered through the labyrinth of rooms, I imagined how astonished Evans must have been as season after season he laid bare more of the palace. Multistoried royal apartments, numerous storerooms, religious shrines, corridors and colonnades, great halls and staircases, light wells, and a grand central court—all were carefully woven into the fabric of the complex. The palace had plumbing. Fresh water was piped in and wastes were flushed out through an elaborate drainage system; some rooms even had baths and toilets.

Minoan tradition endures on Crete, where craftsmen fashion giant clay pots (right) much as their ancestors did more than 3,500 years ago. In ground-floor storage areas in the palace at Knossos, archeologists uncovered rows of such pots, or *pithoi* (left), used to store oil. First in the Aegean to use the potter's wheel, the Minoans excelled in the ceramic arts. They created vibrant, natural designs on fired clay vessels, prized by peoples around the eastern Mediterranean.

Built of masonry and wood, the palace rose as many as five stories and sprawled across more than three acres. Over the years, the architects added new wings and walls, and the Knossos palace grew like a honeycomb. Expansion could have continued, for the palace had no fortifying walls to confine its growth. No walls? How could so rich and powerful a center afford to stand unprotected? Perhaps Minoan fleets were so formidable that Knossos needed no other defense. Or perhaps the Minoans lived in harmony with neighboring peoples and thus feared no attack or invasion.

But there are signs of destruction in the Palace of Minos. As Evans dug deeper, a layer cake of buildings emerged, spanning a period of six centuries. It appeared that earthquakes, which have rocked the Cretan countryside through the ages, had shaken the palace repeatedly. Each time, the Minoans rebuilt the ruined sections. Once, around 1700 B.C., much of the structure was damaged. A remodeled palace was erected—larger and more majestic than before.

That was the Knossos I saw, and that was the last Palace of Minos. For sometime in the early 14th century B.C. Knossos fell to a flaming death. I saw a wall on the west facade that still bears the dark stain of fire. Whose hand lit the torch that burned the palace—and why? If the fire resulted from a natural catastrophe, Minoan society never recovered its strength as it had in the wake of previous disasters. Why had this destruction proved to be more calamitous than before? Archeologists often look to the roots of a civilization for clues to its demise. How did the Minoan civilization begin, and why did it bloom on Crete?

As I traveled around the island, visiting the sites where the Minoans had lived, I recalled a conversation in Athens with Greek archeologist John Sakellarakis. He and his wife, Effie, have excavated for 15 years at a number of Minoan sites. Before I departed for Crete he told me, "Don't look at the villages; look at the countryside—from the sky down. It's the same land the Minoans found. Think about the land, how they saw it and where they lived, and maybe you will see the Minoans."

Crete rises from the sea in a crescendo of mountains that stretch across the narrow face of the island. Down from their jagged peaks they slope and plunge to form valleys and plains where industrious people could settle and thrive.

Today, the land of Crete is harsh and weathered, baked by the sun, shaken by earthquakes, and creased—like the face of an old Cretan peasant—with the traces of a long, rich life. In small villages and countryside farms, the stones of every wall and home seem shaped by the hands of the ancients. Crete looks old.

Yet her face once was not so stern. Forests of cypress, chestnut, pine, and oak blanketed Crete's mountain slopes, sheltering deer, boar, and *agrimia*, or large wild goats. Small rivers and streams flowed through deep gorges, and cool sea breezes tempered the air. It was to this climate that her first people came, and one place they settled was the low knoll of Kephala. Deep beneath the Palace of Minos, archeologists reached a level of soil where these people erected their huts. It is one of the oldest Neolithic settlements in Europe.

The date was around 6100 B.C., and the people were farmers of the New Stone Age. They came to the land by sea, perhaps from the Near East. Some may have traveled north from Libya and Egypt, or south from Greece, for Crete lies at the hub of the eastern Mediterranean, nearly equidistant from Europe, Africa, and Asia.

Along with domestic animals and seeds for their crops, the first settlers brought the skills, traditions, and languages of their forebears. What dialects they may have spoken remains a mystery. But one tradition they carried left a lasting imprint: the worship of nature in the form of female deities, whose blessings ensured bountiful harvests and healthy childbirth—in essence, the survival of the people.

The sea protects Crete like a great moat, and her first people were relatively secure in their island fastness. Still, they lived in small settlements away from the sea. For over the centuries new groups of immigrants steadily reached Crete's shores, and the original inhabitants gradually assimilated them. Then, at the beginning of the third millennium B.C., a quiet revolution took place.

It was the dawn of the Age of Bronze on Crete. A new fertile crescent was forming around the shores of the eastern Mediterranean. From Egypt in the south, up the coast of the Levant to Anatolia in the north, people were moving, and new ideas were spreading.

Crete hung like a jewel in the center of this great arc, and soon the quiet revolution rolled to her shores.

"The Minoan Bronze Age may have been inaugurated by people from some part of the eastern Mediterranean who brought with them, besides metallurgy, new styles of pottery and the custom of burial in domed circular tombs," wrote Sinclair Hood, a noted scholar and former Director of the British School of Archaeology in Athens.

Down to the coast came the peoples of Crete. They established towns near the sea, where good harbors sheltered their ships. With renewed eagerness, they looked to the sea as an avenue of trade and innovation. Population swelled, and new settlements burgeoned. The Bronze Age peoples of Crete had now evolved into the Minoans.

"Crete was perhaps the New World of this time," continued Sinclair Hood, "and the stimulus provided by a mixture of peoples with different traditions and backgrounds may have been responsible for the unique flowering of civilization there. . . ."

At the beginning of the second millennium B.C., the Minoans, in a surge of splendor, erected what have become the hallmarks of their civilization: the palaces. At Knossos and Mallia in the north, at Phaistos in the south, and later at Kato Zakro in the east, the palaces rose in lavish grandeur to proclaim the ascent of Minoan Crete.

As wealth and power amassed, Minoan society became structured and specialized. The Minoans grew ever more vigorous with the excitement of change and the spread of their influence. "The Minoans gathered ideas from Egypt, the Near East, the Cyclades—all around the Mediterranean," American archeologist Steven Diamant told me in Athens. "But they never used an idea exactly as they found it. By the time it passed through their hands, they had made it something uniquely Minoan."

Then, around 1700 B.C., calamity struck the Minoans. Their palaces were severely damaged, probably by a violent earthquake. Seemingly undaunted, the Minoans rebuilt them.

"Life in the Cretan palaces in the Second-palatial period," wrote archeologist Reynold Higgins, formerly Keeper of Greek and Roman Antiquities at the British Museum, "was even more artistic and luxurious than before; goldsmiths, silversmiths, bronze-workers, ivory-workers, seal-engravers, faience-workers, fresco-painters and potters worked for the local rulers to create a culture of a standard which had never been attained before . . . and which would not be seen again for many centuries."

Despite her gray and tumbled ruin of today, Phaistos surely must have stood as the queen of Minoan palaces. Legend says that King Minos's brother, Rhadamanthus, ruled here, that he was a wise and just man and a great lawgiver. After they died, both Minos and Rhadamanthus were appointed judges of the dead in Hades.

I walked up the steps of the grand staircase at Phaistos and stopped to look down on the lands it commanded. Crowning a hill above the verdant plain of Messara, the palace seemed to ride like a ship on the crest of a wave. Rumpled mountains ringed the plain, and the Mediterranean glistened beyond the southern hills.

I entered the open-air central court, a feature common to all Minoan palaces. Nearly 170 feet long, the court was dusty and quiet and empty. Yet this huge plaza with its flagstone floor possibly once captured the gaze of thousands of people who crowded balconies and galleries to witness a dangerous Minoan spectacle: the bull games. With the grace of dancers and the skill of gymnasts, highly trained

Mysterious messages and delicate art survive from Minoan days of glory. Ecstatic women dance in a meadow of flowers *(below)* on an engraved gold ring from a tomb near Knossos. Dressed in flounced skirts and tight, open bodices—the fashion of Minoan noblewomen—they behold a goddess descending from the sky; the scene may portray a ritual in her honor. Women appear as freely and frequently as men in Minoan art. This hints, perhaps, at their important position in Minoan society. Gold serpents twine the arms of an ivory figurine nearly seven inches tall *(right)*—perhaps a snake-cult priestess. In the cult, the snakes may have served as messengers from the underworld. Much of the Minoans' religion and thought puzzles scholars, for they left no texts to explain their beliefs. Archeologists have discovered some 300 examples of a script known as Linear A, but they have not yet deciphered it. The Phaistos Disk (left) embodies one of the most baffling Minoan riddles. Found within the palace complex at Phaistos in 1908, the disk contains 241 pictographs impressed with 45 different stamps—the earliest known example of printing. Yet like many things Minoan, the purpose and the message of the disk remain enigmas.

athletes—both men and women—leaped and tumbled, pranced and dodged, perhaps working to exhaust the great beast in the court. One masterpiece from the Palace of Minos, known as the "Toreador Fresco," illustrates what may have been a bull dancer's most death-defying stunt. With the aid of two teammates, an athlete might grasp the horns of a charging bull and, with the toss of the beast's head, somersault to its back and jump to the ground unharmed. Numerous representations of bull-leaping have been found in frescoes, on seal stones, and in statuettes of ivory and bronze. But the question remains: Why did they do it? Was it sport? Sacrifice? A religious ritual? No one can ever be certain.

The bull, ancient symbol of fertility and strength, appears in all forms of Minoan art and throughout the palaces of Crete. Inside the dark caves where Minoans worshiped, archeologists have found many small bronze and terra-cotta bulls, perhaps placed as votive offerings to a goddess.

Europe's oldest throne, a stark gypsum seat, stands in a low-ceilinged room in the palace at Knossos. Whether Minoans or Mycenaeans—a people from Greece who later displaced the Minoans—ruled from this throne remains unknown.

The Minoans were not people obsessed with dying and cults of the dead. They worshiped life and the forces of nature that controlled earth, sea, and sky. This is evident in their art, both in the choice of subjects from nature—birds, flowers, trees, marine life—and in the graceful naturalism with which they were rendered.

Yet the Minoans, despite their artistic traditions, seem to have had no sense of history. Archeologists are left with vexing problems. Who were the leaders, the heroes, and what did they do? The Minoans offer us no names, no dates. Even Minos has come to us through myth, and the word may have been merely a title.

"It's so hard to bring them from the tombs to the flesh," Greek archeologist Effie Sakellarakis told me. In 1965 she and her husband, John, discovered the first undisturbed noble burial on Crete—the skeleton of a woman bedecked with gold jewelry. Over the years John and Effie have worked at a variety of Minoan sites, from tombs to palaces. "Digging gives you a better idea of the details of daily life," Effie explained. "It's like unlocking a room that someone left in a hurry. After a day of digging I go home and think about the things we found and try to get a feeling for the people who left them."

What sense, I wondered, do the Minoans convey? "Joy," said Effie. "The joy of life."

But all their zest for life did not help the Minoans, and their world came to an end. The Minoans themselves left no comprehensible record to help us understand their fate. For one of the enduring enigmas of the Minoan civilization lies in their written language. It remains undeciphered. In fact, not one, but four writing systems have been discovered at Minoan sites. The first, a hieroglyphic style, bears a vague resemblance to that of Egypt. From this, the scratchy script known as Linear A evolved, and it became the primary system used by Minoan palace scribes. The third is embodied in a single mysterious artifact known as the Phaistos Disk. When archeologists found it at the Phaistos palace complex in 1908, they soon detected its most remarkable feature. The 241 pictograph signs had been impressed in the clay with 45 different stamps. It is the earliest known example of printing, but its message is unknown.

The fourth script is not Minoan. Known as Linear B, this writing was first found on tablets at Knossos and dated from the palace's last years. Archeologists reasoned that it had replaced Linear A as the palace script. Other caches of Linear B tablets were found on mainland Greece, and it was soon determined that it was the script of the Mycenaeans, not the Minoans.

Did warriors from Mycenae, then, step ashore and subdue the powerful Minoans of Crete? Quite possibly. But perhaps it was more than the hand of man that ended the reign of King Minos.

A sleeping dragon lurks beneath the wine-dark waters north of Crete. It lives deep within the small Aegean island of Thera, 70 miles from Knossos. Now and then, when it sighs, black smoke spews from Thera, and the people are frightened. Some flee the island.

The dragon is a mighty, seething volcano whose cone once rose to a lofty peak in the center of Thera. The island was round as a coin, with rich soil and pleasant harbors. Minoan ships called at a port, now named Akrotiri, on Thera's south coast; the island itself may have been under the Minoan sphere of influence.

Sometime around 1500 B.C., when the Minoan civilization seemed at its sparkling zenith, Thera's dragon awoke with fiery vengeance. Belching ash and hot pumice high into the air, the mountain erupted, possibly several times over a period of years, in what many scientists believe to be one of the most violent series of volcanic events known to man.

After blasting out its molten interior, Thera's volcano collapsed, leaving the island a crescent-shaped shell. As the cone slumped beneath the sea, enormous tidal waves began to roll. Crete probably lay in their path. Volcanic ash blackened the skies above the eastern Mediterranean, and along its shores people no doubt trembled with fear and begged their gods for mercy.

In recent years, a number of archeologists have connected this great cataclysm and the subsequent "disappearance" of the Minoan civilization with the ancient myth of Atlantis—Plato's tale of a beautiful, civilized island that suddenly and mysteriously sank beneath the waves. Although the myth of a lost island appears in other cultures, it is possible that the memory of this disaster inspired the Greek version of the Atlantis myth.

As if fired by lava bombs from Thera's explosion, every Minoan center but one suffered flaming destruction about 1450 B.C.; only the Palace of Minos was spared. But Thera's volcano—70 miles away—could not have burned the palaces and towns of Crete. And why was Phaistos, far down on the south coast, abandoned forever, while Knossos, facing the source of cataclysm, thrived for another 75 years?

The mystery surrounding the end of Minoan Crete provokes heated debate among scholars. In 1939 the late Greek archeologist Spyridon Marinatos published the theory that Thera's eruption brought ruin to the Minoan civilization. Then, in 1967, he began to unearth the port town of Akrotiri on Thera's south coast, preserved like a Minoan Pompeii beneath tons of volcanic debris. The inhabitants apparently had deserted the town just before the first eruption.

Brushing dirt from a potsherd, a worker sorts bones and artifacts at a Minoan cemetery near Arkhanes, south of Knossos. In 1965 archeologists found here the first unplundered noble burial on Crete: the remains of a Minoan woman adorned with gold jewelry.

It is possible, then, that the Minoans were destroyed by the very powers of nature they worshiped.

Yet since Marinatos first proposed this theory, scholars have presented numerous variations on his original idea for a simple, important reason. The evidence does not match up. If the Minoans were destroyed as Marinatos suggests, why did Knossos survive?

The presence of Linear B tablets in Minos's palace hints at a takeover by the Mycenaeans of mainland Greece. For while Minoan Crete flourished in peaceful grandeur, the Mycenaeans had grown steadily more powerful. Many scholars believe that the Minoans gradually were absorbed by the Mycenaeans. Perhaps the Mycenaeans occupied the Palace of Minos as their Cretan headquarters after Thera's eruption. Then, sometime early in the 14th century B.C., the palace was burned, and Knossos fell. Who was the enemy, and who the defender? Perhaps, in rebellion against the Mycenaeans, it was the Minoans themselves who burned the palace. Perhaps not.

When Arthur Evans excavated the Palace of Minos, he found an extraordinary room during his first season of excavation. Against a wall decorated with frescoes of wingless griffins stood a regal gypsum chair. It may be Europe's first throne. With a dab of truth and a splash of fancy, archeologist J. D. S. Pendlebury once imagined the last act of a falling king in this room.

"The final scene takes place in the most dramatic room ever excavated—the Throne Room. It was found in a state of complete confusion. A great oil jar lay overturned in one corner, ritual vessels were in the act of being used when the disaster came. It looks as if the king had been hurried here to undergo too late some last ceremony in the hopes of saving the people."

Whether or not the Mycenaeans displaced the Minoans, a great civilization vanished into oblivion. But legacies from the Minoan world lingered. "The Greeks looked back with reverence to Crete," writes Greek archeologist Nicolaos Platon. "From Crete came their supreme god Zeus; from Crete came much of the ancient wisdom that was to inspire their philosophers. From Crete, too, came the basis of their legal system and the great tradition of wise and incorruptible judges—a tradition which is both a historical fact and a time-honoured legend stretching back to one of the oldest of the Greek myths: the appointment of Minos and Rhadamanthus, after their death, as judges of the dead in the underworld."

Once again I stood at the mouth of the Gorge of the Dead. Up the steep walls were the caves where early Minoans had buried their dead. Below the gorge on the fertile plain by the sea, the ruins of Kato Zakro shone white in the hot sun. Only in 1962 did Nicolaos Platon uncover its crumbled walls. Surely other great ruins lie sealed in the rocky soil of Crete, and their discovery may help solve the riddles that haunt the rise and fall of Europe's first civilization.

Who were the Minoans? Perhaps one day we shall know. For with each new discovery we move closer to understanding them. Perhaps we shall see beyond their eyes into their minds. Even so, they have left us something more important. As the traditions of their ancestors lived with them, so their traditions still live with us. In a sense we are all the heirs of Minos.

Evening mist swathes a valley beyond the ruins of Phaistos (opposite), second in size of the four excavated Minoan palaces. In the distance rises the saddleback peak of Ida, Crete's

highest mountain, once held sacred by Minoans. Above, boxing children spar again as a restorer assembles fragments of a Minoan-style fresco from Akrotiri, a site on Thera.

Pilgrimage of fear: Bearing gifts to appease angry gods, Minoans climb to a sanctuary atop Mount Juktas, a sacred peak near Knossos, as smoke from Thera's

volcano mushrooms above the horizon. In the shrine, a priestess raises a votive figurine before casting it into a crevice, perhaps in the hope that this offering will help calm the earth. Although ash blanketed much of Crete, experts still debate the eruption's lasting effects on the island.

 alm waters engulf a slumbering giant beneath the cliffside town of Thera. Ships roll gently in the island's deep bay, actually the flooded caldera

of the ancient volcano. A dark island in the center of the bay still periodically steams and spews lava, marking the spot where a lofty mountain once exploded. Several eruptions, perhaps some of the worst witnessed by man, may have weakened the brilliant Minoan civilization.

MYCENAEANS: WARRIOR-

by CYNTHIA RUSS RAMSAY   photographed by GORDON W. GAHAN

MERCHANTS OF GREECE

A ll their might and splendor could not save them. A tide of violence overwhelmed the powerful warriors and destroyed their towns, then the richest in all of Europe. Fires blackened walled citadels and consumed shrines and workshops. Great palace-centers like Mycenae, Tiryns, and Pylos fell to ruin. People fled—the courtly ladies in flounced skirts, the tall men bearing shields and bronze swords, the merchants who traded in wine and perfumed oil. In the ensuing chaos arts declined, and the knowledge of writing disappeared. By the 12th century B.C., a great civilization had perished. It had prospered for about 400 years in southern and central Greece, and then it was gone. No one really knows how. Or why.

Greek myths and the epic poems of Homer preserved a vague memory of that distant heroic age. But in time the words lost their link to the historical past, and the civilization faded into legend.

By the 19th century, most scholars dismissed the story of the *Iliad*—the expedition to rescue beautiful Helen from the citadel of Troy—as pure invention. They even doubted that Troy ever existed. But Heinrich Schliemann, a German-born merchant, contended that Homer's tales portrayed history.

Virtually no one agreed with the eccentric self-taught scholar and self-made millionaire. So determined was he to prove the truth of the storied exploits of ancient heroes in bronze armor that he retired from business in his early 40's and set out to find evidence for Homer's world.

And find it he did. By luck or by genius, Schliemann uncovered what many believe is the fabled city of Troy. Starting in 1870, he made a series of excavations in a hill on the coast of western Turkey. He found a town that had been rebuilt time after time for 2,000 years, one house constructed atop the rubble of the previous one.

Despite his achievement, Schliemann initially misjudged and miscalculated. He mistakenly identified one of the deepest levels as the Troy of Homer; those remains were actually more than a thousand years older than he realized. The triumph of discovery, however, remains his to this day.

A far greater discovery awaited him in Greece. In 1876 he astonished the world with sensational finds from royal graves inside the citadel of Mycenae. Nineteen skeletons had been interred with vast riches: burial masks and jewelry of hammered gold; ornaments of amber, rock crystal, and ivory; inlaid daggers and swords.

But Schliemann found more than this dazzling treasure. He unearthed proof of a civilization that had vanished beneath the rocky soil and debris of more than 30 centuries. Until Schliemann, few people in modern times had suspected that Greece, long before the age of Socrates and Plato, had been home to a culture of great wealth and sophistication.

In the century since Schliemann brought Homer's legendary golden Mycenae to life, the prodigious labors of scholars have drawn into sharper focus the civilization we now call Mycenaean. The name applies not only to the one site but also to a uniform style of art and way of life that prevailed across much of southern Greece from the 16th century to the 12th century B.C.

"We know who they were, where they were, and when they

Overleaf: Helmeted warriors fight to the death in an engraving on the face of a gold seal ring, less than an inch and a half across. The ornament, part of a fabulous treasure recovered from royal graves at the ruins of Mycenae, dates to the 16th century B.C., when a great civilization began to emerge on the mainland of Greece.

were," said John Younger, one of the archeologists who led me into the past. "We know that their merchants and kings grew rich on overseas trade; that their architects designed great vaulted stone tombs and palaces with pillars and frescoed walls; that their engineers built roads, bridges, fortresses, and elaborate drainage systems; that their sculptors and painters, potters and weavers created works of great beauty; and that their officials and clerks kept state records and inventories inscribed on clay tablets in a script called Linear B.

"But in spite of all we have learned," said John, a professor at Duke University in North Carolina, "we are still seeking answers to the very perplexing question of what caused the civilization to collapse abruptly and violently."

With those words in mind, I set out on my journey in search of the Mycenaeans and clues to their strange, turbulent demise. I arrived in Greece in summer, when oleanders bloom and brighten the roadsides with pink, when cicadas sing, and when grass turns golden in the heat. It is also the season when archeologists and their students leave their classrooms and begin to excavate.

My quest took me southwest from Athens across a hilly landscape never far from the sighing of the sea. In the cloudless days that followed, I met several archeologists, dedicated people who, with care and patience, attempt to wring information from the earth.

George E. Mylonas, a Greek-American, was one of these. Retired from Washington University in St. Louis, *(Continued on page 152)*

From imposing palace-towns on the Peloponnesus of southern Greece, Mycenaean influence slowly expanded throughout the Aegean. Shrewd traders and forceful warriors, the Mycenaeans overspread the Cyclades and Crete, and their culture soon prevailed. At the zenith of their power—about 1250 B.C.—the seafaring Mycenaeans may have coursed the eastern Mediterranean from Sicily to Turkey.

147

Citadel of Mycenae, an awesome fortress more than 3,000 years old, crowns a sun-washed hill in southern Greece. Below the ruins of the

palace-town, sheep graze on the Argive Plain. Farming and herding formed the basis of Mycenaean subsistence. But far-ranging Mycenaean merchants also traded pottery and olive oil for copper and tin—both metals vital to the making of bronze tools and weapons.

ourners at the funeral of a warrior-prince lament, while the bereaved mother cuts a lock of her hair to place on the corpse. The

*family will arrange a treasure of gifts around the body after lowering it into the grave's shaft.
Such graves, dating from the 16th century B.C., sheltered the riches until archeologists discovered
the tombs about a hundred years ago and began bringing to light the world of the Mycenaeans.*

Missouri, he is now vice-president of the prestigious Academy of Athens. At a vigorous 80 years of age, he continues to work at Mycenae where he has excavated every summer since 1950.

In June, early morning is the best time to visit Mycenae, before the air quivers with heat and before the crowds of tourists arrive to distract from its antiquity. Only the braying of donkeys broke the silence as I left the present-day village of Mycenae, a scant two miles from the ruins. Ahead, to the right, the ancient citadel hunched on a hilltop, gray and somber in the opalescent light. It is still defended by the famed Cyclopean walls, built of rectangular stones so large that later Greeks believed only the Cyclopes, mythical one-eyed giants, could have put them in place.

I felt a prickle of excitement as I approached the citadel's high bastions and huge entrance gate, guarded by two stone lions. Headless now, these figures still emanate an aura of power. Standing below them, I could imagine how the Lion Gate had awed all who entered—the nobles and their subjects, the artisans and workers who flocked to Mycenae.

All would come to pay homage and taxes to their warrior-king and to worship in the cult center. And if fighting flared between Mycenae and other towns, they would come to find safety, perhaps jostling each other in their haste.

I met Professor Mylonas inside the gate, and together we walked past the ruins of the guardroom and granary, past the graves where Schliemann had found such great treasure, to the town's religious sanctuary. As Mylonas described them, the ravaged buildings,

Reconstruction of ancient Mycenae reveals the imposing appearance of the citadel. On the crest of the acropolis rose the palace, its megaron, or great central hall, richly decorated with frescoes and painted floors and ceilings. Sanctuaries, royal workshops and storerooms, and the dwellings of nobles lined the hill below the palace. Outside the citadel walls and on adjacent hillsides stood the houses of merchants and factories for the production of perfumed oil.

LISA BIGANZOLI

shrines, and altars became scenes of piety. Religious processions, led by priests in rich, flowing robes, descended from the palace along a grand stairway. Soon the altars turned red with the blood of bulls; libations of honey, olive oil, and wine flowed from ornate sacred vessels; and sad-eyed terra-cotta figurines stared from niches where, Professor Mylonas believes, they were placed to ward off evil.

"Until the excavations of 1968, we didn't know the religious area existed. Its discovery illustrates one of the principles of archeology: If you don't find it, it doesn't mean that it's not there."

On the brow of the hill above the sanctuary rose the royal palace. Remnants of walls marked the outlines of main halls and smaller rooms, all now open to the sky. I stood in the early-morning stillness. Only the rising sun warmed the great circular hearth in the center of the throne room. Weeds sprouted where once nobles had assembled to drink wine and to feast around the fire.

I closed my eyes and blotted out the radiant Aegean morning, letting my imagination slip back across the centuries. Smoke drifted through the room, giant flames licked at the darkness, and frescoes with scenes of the hunt and of court life glimmered in the trembling light. A great king lifted his golden wine cup and for the moment banished thoughts of impending strife.

For the Mycenaeans were haunted by fear beginning about the middle of the 13th century B.C. Scholars dispute what menaced them, but it is clear that suddenly defenses were strengthened in palace centers across Greece.

Professor Mylonas showed me walls that had been rebuilt and enlarged. I followed a stairway down to a hidden cistern where the uneasy rulers had secured Mycenae's water supply in the event of a long siege. Mycenae had been vulnerable because it lacked sufficient water on the acropolis itself. To remedy this, engineers cut a long, low passage beneath the fortress wall and dug a tunnel leading to an underground water supply outside the citadel. In this way, a beleaguered population could fetch water without being seen. Such cisterns have also been found at Tiryns and Athens.

"Just what was it that these people feared so much?" I asked Professor Mylonas.

"I believe they feared local uprisings," he answered crisply. "Murders within the royal family could have fomented a civil war—and that can be the most destructive kind of war there is.

"Look at Mycenae's walls. When men are fighting with arrows, spears, and swords, the only way to take such a fortress is by surprise attack. That was not likely, since the citadel stands on a hill overlooking the countryside, and the roads were guarded. So there must have been some sort of internal struggle that provoked the fall."

To help explain his theory, Professor Mylonas turned to tradition for clues. He believes that tales of the murder of the Mycenaean king Agamemnon upon his return from the Trojan War and the revenge that followed echo actual episodes in the struggle for power. The long absence of the leader apparently weakened authority at home and invited conspiracy among nobles. Ambition and jealousy ignited by opportunity touched off plots and counterplots that soon devastated the land and brought the Mycenaean civilization to a shuddering halt.

"I'm convinced the legends contain at least a kernel of history. After all, why would succeeding generations invent stories about this place, which by Homer's time had become simply a minor town?"

Tiryns, another citadel some ten miles to the south, shared the same sad fate as Mycenae. Not even fortress walls 50 feet thick in places could save it from destruction.

I made the short journey across the Argive Plain in time to find Joachim Weisshaar, a blond and brawny German archeologist, supervising a crew of laborers at an excavation site just outside the citadel walls. We were standing before the remains of a Mycenaean village that survived after the citadel of Tiryns had been abandoned. The archeologist's spade, I learned, is mostly in the hands of students and

Called treasure hunter by some and father of Aegean archeology by others, Heinrich Schliemann astounded the world with his discovery of Mycenaean grandeur. Using ancient historical accounts and the epic poems of Homer as guides, Schliemann excavated five royal shaft graves at Mycenae in 1876. He found a hoard of treasure there that echoed Homer's description of a city "rich in gold."

Golden burial mask
(left) preserves the
haughty countenance of a
bearded noble buried in
one of the shaft graves at
Mycenae. Schliemann
called it the mask of
Agamemnon after the
leader of Greek forces in
the Iliad, Homer's epic
of the Trojan War. But the
portrait dates to the dawn
of the Mycenaean era,
some 300 years before the
war could have taken
place. Another burial
mask (right) captures the
wry smile of a Mycenaean
aristocrat. A profile
incised on an amethyst
bead less than half an
inch in diameter records
the features of still
another Mycenaean. The
shaft graves of Mycenae
produced amazing
riches—cups, vases,
jewelry, and hundreds of
ornaments of gold, as well
as masterpieces in ivory,
silver, and precious
stones. Scholars puzzle
over how the Mycenaeans
accumulated so much so
quickly. Some theorize
that they gained their
wealth as plunder in war
or as payment for
mercenary action in
Egypt. Others attribute it
to their abilities as
shrewd traders. Whatever
the answer, something
dramatic happened to
create the first surge of
prosperity that set the
Mycenaeans on the road
to a dynamic civilization.

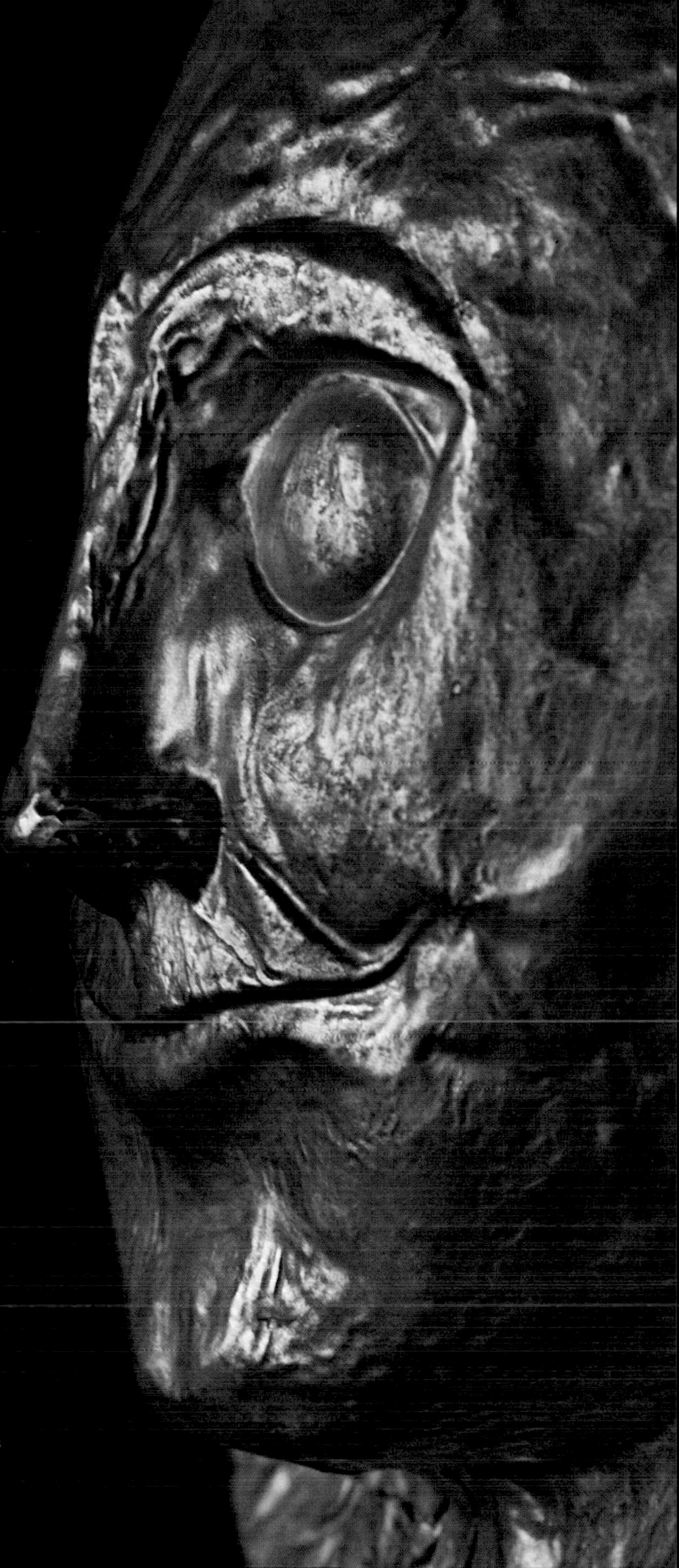

local villagers, who fill their slack time between summer and fall harvest seasons by digging up the past. The archeologist, in turn, keeps more than busy recording the exact location of what is found.

"A good archeologist," Joachim said, "should be able to replace artifacts and to reconstruct a site in the way he found it. Otherwise, you dig through the evidence and demolish it forever."

Stakes in the ground formed a grid that divided the area into square-meter sections. "The contents of every square meter every five to eight centimeters down go into a separate basket," explained Joachim. "Pottery is the mainstay of the collection. In one year we collect anywhere from 100,000 to 300,000 shards. But what we record and study is the painted pottery—the luxury ware used by the upper classes. This accounts for only 15 percent of our finds."

Joachim handed me a potsherd no larger than a half dollar and mumbled, "Late Helladic III C."

I knew enough to realize that this referred to a late style of Mycenaean painted pottery crafted between 1220 and 1170 B.C. Since the great catalog of vase motifs and shapes was organized and published by the Swedish scholar Arne Furumark, pottery has provided the basis for Mycenaean chronology—to those who can read it. Still, I am continuously amazed at the ability of archeologists to pick up a small fragment of a pot, and from the color, texture, bit of design, curvature, length of stem, or flex of lip deduce the style and date of the piece.

One archeologist used an analogy to explain his expertise. "If you had a keen interest in automobiles, for instance, and you noted the changes in car features year after year, you could construct a similar chronology. The 1930's might be identified by the distinctive streamlined shape of car bodies then."

Late in the day, after the workmen had departed, Joachim and I slowly walked up the entrance ramp to Tiryns. Our ascent put us in the direct line of fire from the twin towers at the main gate. No arrows or javelins impeded our climb, but even in the honey-gold light of the afternoon, I found Tiryns an unwelcoming place. The rampart looked like a stone grimace against the azure sky.

"You don't need walls like this for defense," Joachim said. "Enemies couldn't take a wall even ten feet thick. So why build a wall of 50 feet? These were meant to impress and to intimidate, to make people living nearby feel that the citadel was impregnable from any kind of attack."

Joachim shares the view of many scholars who believe that the Mycenaean civilization was struck down by revolution and intrigue from within.

The respected American scholar Rhys Carpenter, on the other hand, contends that climatic change was the major contributing cause of such uprisings. Professor Carpenter propounded an ingenious theory, which has intrigued many of his colleagues, in a series of lectures in 1965 and in a book entitled *Discontinuity in Greek Civilization*. He argued that persistent drought created widespread famine—a crisis that might have proved fatal to Mycenaean authority. Perhaps desperate men, driven by hunger, toppled thrones in a series of peasant revolts.

Carefully joined stone blocks form a corbeled dome that soars more than 40 feet high in the Treasury of Atreus, a burial chamber at Mycenae. Perhaps the finest example of Mycenaean engineering and architecture, this beehive-shaped tholos tomb once had an elaborate columned entrance and bronze rosettes adorning its walls. More accessible than the earlier shaft graves, tholos tombs often fell prey to robbers; nothing remains at Mycenae of the lavish tribute left in the graves of royalty.

A new field of study called palynology, which enables scientists to reconstruct the flora and climate of ages past from pollen particles mixed in the soil, may ultimately provide evidence for such a severe and lengthy drought. But for the present most scholars do not wholly accept climatic change as the prime cause of the collapse of Mycenaean civilization.

Most experts also question the traditional theory that destruction was brought on by waves of Dorian-speaking invaders from the north looking for places to settle. These people, who were important in Greece later, simply may have begun to populate lands that the Mycenaeans could no longer control.

Archeologists like Joachim Weisshaar ask, "How could groups of nomads encumbered with families and flocks storm such citadels? How could strongholds be attacked by foreigners who left absolutely no trace?"

For not a single knife blade, not a single potsherd from any identifiable foreign conqueror has ever been found among the ruins. In centers such as Mycenae and Tiryns, life, though changed, resumed after the sounds of revolution had died away. It lingered, however, for only a few decades longer.

Relatively few areas in the Mycenaean realm weathered the catastrophes. Of the 224 known sites in southern Greece, only 35 continued to be occupied into the 12th century B.C. Pylos, a palace-

ti ri po de、 ai   ke   u、 ke re si   jo、 we ke   2

TWO TRIPOD . . . CALDRONS OF CRETAN TYPE

Inscribed in Linear B, a script that combines symbolic characters and pictographs, the clay tablet (top) from the palace archives at Pylos records an inventory of pots, wine jars, and goblets. Early investigators thought that each of the some 90 symbols represented a syllable of either a vowel or a consonant and a vowel. But it took the inspiration of Michael Ventris to break the syllabic code in 1952. By a complex cryptographic process, he discovered the sounds of the symbols. These revealed that the language read as an archaic form of Greek. Scholars then translated the Greek into English. The above tablet, unearthed after Ventris had completed his work, helped confirm his decipherment. The word *tiripo* refers to the symbols above it and to the pictograph of a three-legged pot.

town to the southwest of Mycenae, was engulfed in flames and abandoned. The raging fire that destroyed the throne room, warehouses, wine storerooms, and workshops also baked the clay tablets in the palace archives, preserving the accounts that scribes kept more than 3,000 years ago.

The 1,200 tablets from Pylos and the scattering of others recovered from different palaces were incised in the script called Linear B—the same script found on the remains of some 3,000 tablets unearthed years before from the palace at Knossos on Crete. This unknown language baffled experts for half a century. Then in 1952 Michael Ventris, an English architect and amateur philologist, deciphered the strange symbols and surprised the world with evidence that Linear B was an early form of Greek. Today, virtually all experts agree with him.

This feat of scholarship rewrote Aegean prehistory with one stroke. It brought Greeks into Greece more than 400 years earlier than many scholars had believed. It demolished the theory that Minoans had colonized the mainland; instead, it put Mycenaeans into the palaces of Crete. It also shattered the image of Mycenaeans as merely roughhewn warlords and buccaneers, for the tablets offer a picture of merchants and bureaucrats highly organized to promote trade.

The tablets, with their records of produce, their lists of bronze, wool, ivory, and other raw materials issued to craftsmen, and their notations of payments made, reveal that the palaces maintained tight control over production in the villages and settlements.

Written in the last months before the fall of Pylos, the tablets also hint at unsettled times. Professor John Chadwick, a Cambridge University philologist who collaborated with Ventris, told me of an entry ordering officials to collect "temple bronze" to make points for spears and javelins.

"This seems to indicate that the monarch at Pylos was taking steps to improve his fighting strength in face of a metal shortage. The king may have feared an enemy attack from the sea. We have documents, sometimes called the mobilization tablets, that list men under the heading 'Thus the watchers are guarding the coastal regions.' And another tablet lists rowers going to Pleuron, possibly a town to the north."

"Who were the raiders that the people of Pylos seemed to fear so much?" I asked.

Professor Chadwick, an amiable gentleman and a cautious scholar, carefully formulated his reply. "We have no real evidence beyond the hints in the tablets that they came from the sea. But if I allow myself to speculate, it is hard to dismiss from my mind the two attacks on Egypt launched in 1225 and 1183 B.C. by a league of mixed tribes known as the Sea Peoples. At about this time the Hittites in Anatolia also suffered before the assaults of these roving bands of raiders and their deadly fleets. Perhaps the Sea Peoples also brought Pylos and other parts of the Mycenaean world to their end.

"In any event, all the eastern Mediterranean appears to have been in turmoil. That trade was disrupted would square with the need to use temple bronze for the armament industry."

In exchange for imports of metal, the Mycenaeans, I learned, exported pottery and olive oil.

It was something of a shock to the late Professor Carl Blegen, the eminent American archeologist who directed the excavation of Pylos in the 1950's, to discover more than 7,500 pottery cups, bowls, and vases in the pantries of the palace at Pylos. He wrote some years later that he found it difficult ". . . to think of the monarch who resided in this great palace with its stately Throne Room . . . as a seller of plain simple domestic pots and pans."

Professor Blegen's assistants counted 2,853 stems of broken goblets, all retrieved from a single room. This prompted Blegen to write: "It is clear from the epic poems that . . . no occasion was ever missed for pouring a libation and having a drink; the vast number of broken fragments . . . led us to believe that after the wine was drunk the kylix [goblet] was thrown to the floor or against the wall and shattered."

Yet the fact remains that all across the Near East, in Syria, Palestine, southern Turkey, and Egypt, and to the west in Italy and Sicily, there are finds of exquisitely decorated Mycenaean pottery. Perhaps Professor Blegen's interpretation was an effort to endow the fragments of pottery and bare masonry with a bit of humanity.

Although the artifacts and ruins recall nothing of laughter and joy, surely the Mycenaeans appreciated mellow wine, fine meals, and good conversation. As I sat in a tavern by the sun-spangled sea, I shared with the Mycenaeans the time-honored pleasure of dining in agreeable company.

I had come to the modern town of Pylos from the nearby excavation site at Voidhokoilia with Professor George Korres of the University of Athens. He was then directing a dig at a tholos tomb—a burial chamber with a beehive-shaped dome. In such tombs, which were often built into hillsides, Mycenaeans buried their dead when the earlier shaft graves went out of style.

Professor Korres, an intense and energetic man, talked about the prosperity of the Mycenaeans.

"At first we thought only the palace-town of Mycenae was rich in gold. But much gold and new treasures have been found recently in a shaft grave and the tholos tombs of Peristeria just north of here. We can only guess at how the Mycenaeans acquired gold in the early stages. The late Professor Spyridon Marinatos believed that the Mycenaeans, famed as warriors, were recruited as mercenaries to serve in Egypt. In addition to gold, he maintained, the Mycenaeans brought back from Egypt the custom of using burial masks.

"But I don't believe the current evidence supports his contentions," Korres said. "I think the wealth, even in the beginning, came from trade. The Mycenaeans seem to have had a monopoly on perfumed olive oil and unguents."

I must have looked a little surprised, because Professor Korres quickly continued, "Remember the ancients had no soap to cleanse themselves. So they applied the oil as a perfume and also used it as a cosmetic for the skin."

Mycenaean power grew quickly for the first two hundred years. By the end of the 15th century B.C. the Greeks had gained strongholds

Roughhewn gallery underlies a mighty wall as thick as 50 feet at the citadel of Tiryns. In the 13th century B.C., at the height of their power, the Mycenaeans suddenly began to strengthen fortifications in many of their palace-towns. The monarchs apparently feared an attack, but by whom remains a mystery. Civil war may have threatened the civilization, or foreign raiders may have harassed trade and invaded towns.

on Crete. But at the time the Mycenaeans took over the palace at Knossos, they had been following many Minoan art styles for more than a century and a half.

"Without Crete, there would have been no Mycenaean art as we know it," explains Professor Emily Vermeule, a highly respected art historian and archeologist at Harvard University. "Every student of the art of shaft graves has tried to distinguish the objects imported from Crete, the imitations made by the Mycenaeans, and the hybrids of various degree."

As the Mycenaeans grew richer, they may have employed Minoan craftsmen to create the new luxuries they craved. "But it probably never took a Greek very long to learn anything," Professor Vermeule observes, "and one or two generations were ample time for the Mycenaeans to perfect their own techniques."

Other archeologists believe that the wealth of the shaft graves at Mycenae came from piracy and plunder, and that only as Minoan power waned did the Mycenaeans turn to trade.

The Cyclades, the central islands of the Aegean, lay along the ancient trade routes from Greece to Crete. Kea, about 12 miles east of the mainland, is one of these islands. By ferry, I sailed to this tiny but historically important bit of land.

The ancient settlement at Ayia Irini on Kea stands on the far side of the bay from the little harbor of Korissia. A sinuous road follows the shore, winding past crescent beaches and a sea so blue that it pierces the eye. Beyond the beaches rise hills studded with olive trees. As I drove around a bend, I swerved past an elderly woman in black, riding sidesaddle on a donkey. She stared at me impassively.

At Ayia Irini, the pottery reflects the shift of power in the Aegean, for Mycenaean wares almost completely replaced Minoan ones by the 14th century.

"Be careful not to infer anything beyond the fact that Kea had contact with the mainland," cautioned Jack Davis, a youthful archeologist from the University of Illinois at Chicago Circle. We walked through the sprawling excavation site to the laboratory where Professor John Caskey, of the University of Cincinnati, and his staff were at work. Two archeologists on the porch were making "joins," finding pieces of pottery that belonged together.

"There are many ways to account for the presence of Mycenaean pottery here," Jack continued. "Consider, for instance, how a cup might have ended up in the location where we found it. It could have come by trade or have been brought back by someone as a gift or souvenir. It didn't have to come from the hand of a conqueror. At one time, invasion was used to explain the presence of all unexpected artifacts. But here that presence could very well have been the result of trade."

The prevailing wind from the north easily could have carried the ancient ships in a day from Kea to the island of Melos, where archeologists recently found a Mycenaean sanctuary. Another day's sail would have taken the ships to the island of Thera and from there on to Crete and Egypt.

Instead of following this route, I returned to the mainland, to the exuberant vitality of Athens. Over tiny cups of strong Turkish coffee, I talked with Demetrius Schilardi and his American wife, Alexis, about their work on Paros, another island in the Cyclades. The excavations—sponsored by the Greek Archaeological Society and the National Geographic Society—show a Mycenaean connection similar to that of the other islands.

"We have also found evidence of widespread destruction," Demetrius said. "It seems the entire eastern Mediterranean was locked in some fierce struggle. Trade suffered and declined, for there was a disruption of contact between the Aegean and the Near East. This proved fatal to the Mycenaean world, which must have depended on imports of raw materials to supply its craftsmen. The Mycenaeans were rich, but without trade their lifeblood drained away."

As I walked to the National Archaeological Museum after leaving the Schilardis, I reflected on the trail of calamity that I had followed across southern Greece.

I had encountered many theories that sought to explain the disintegration of the Mycenaean world. Did prolonged drought bring ruin? Was the downfall caused by pirates who swarmed across the eastern Mediterranean, plundering towns and hampering trade? Or was it the work of treacherous nobles who embroiled the palace centers in bloody plots?

Inside the museum I lingered in front of showcases filled with the dazzling treasures of the Mycenaeans. Though these relics have not dispelled the mystery, their very presence proves that a civilization once believed to be legendary truly existed. Whatever snuffed out their world, the Mycenaeans—through their works of art, their skillfully fashioned artifacts—have found immortality.

LYVIA BROWN

"One of the most compelling works of art yet recovered from the Mycenaean world," says archeologist Colin Renfrew of the nearly 18-inch-tall ceramic cult figure he found at a sanctuary on the island of Melos.

Artwork and artifacts reveal the aggressive military spirit of the Mycenaeans, who prided themselves on skill in warfare and in the hunt. Inlaid with gold and silver, a dagger blade (below) recovered from a shaft grave shows warriors armed with javelins and bows pursuing lions. Early royal tombs often contained a rich assortment of daggers and swords, some with ornate handles and blades. The bronze cuirass, or body armor, from a warrior's tomb gives support to

Homer's description in the Iliad of "... the strength of armoured men in bronze...." Homer also refers to leather helmets covered with a protective layer of boars' tusks. A massacre of unidentified men dressed in animal skins inspired a fresco (upper right) found in the charred rubble of the palace at Pylos. The painting on a nearly 16-inch-high vase of the early 12th century B.C. indicates that the Mycenaeans' fascination with war persisted into the waning years of their civilization. "It would almost seem as if they loved strife for its own sake," observed Lord William Taylour, who has excavated in the Aegean for 25 years.

FROM "THE PALACE OF NESTOR AT PYLOS IN WESTERN MESSENIA, VOL. II," BY MABEL L. LANG, REPRINTED BY PERMISSION OF PRINCETON UNIVERSITY PRESS AND UNIVERSITY OF CINCINNATI (ABOVE); EKDOTIKE ATHENON S.A., NATIONAL ARCHAEOLOGICAL MUSEUM, ATHENS (BOTH, BELOW)

ock-crystal bowl in the form of a duck reflects
the refined taste of warrior-kings who buried
their wealth in shaft graves at Mycenae. Not

until the 13th century B.C., with Greek influence burgeoning in the Mediterranean, did Mycenaean centers reach the peak of their prosperity and power. In the 12th century, when trade faltered in the wake of violence and upheaval, the mighty civilization collapsed.

ETRUSCANS: FESTIVE IN LIFE, LAVISH IN DEATH

by JUDITH E. RINARD

photographed by JAMES P. BLAIR

Down a dark passageway I slowly descended, groping my way between ancient stone walls. Before me, a guide carried a lamp that bobbed in the gloom and cast flickering shadows on the cold walls. With each hesitating step, I was penetrating farther into the Tomb of the Leopards, an Etruscan crypt deep in a lonely hillside in Italy, about 45 miles northwest of Rome.

In this tomb and in others scattered nearby, the Etruscans, obscure predecessors of the Romans, had buried their dead some 2,500 years ago, placing them in spacious chambers laboriously carved from solid rock. And in several of the tombs, including this one, I knew that the Etruscans had painted scenes of their strange and luxurious life, a life that faded away about the time Jesus was born. Here, I hoped to find at last some tangible picture of the elusive people that I was seeking.

I had looked first for their ancient city of Tarquinia on the rolling, windswept plain above me. The Italians call this land the Maremma—the coastal moor. There, on a quiet hillside, Tarquinia once had stood, a proud citadel overlooking the Tyrrhenian Sea. Today, a town near the site bears the name of Tarquinia. But of the ancient Etruscan city I had seen not one building. Its great temples and homes, built mostly of wood and decorated with terra-cotta, have long since perished. Only bare stone foundations remain. Except for these, there is nothing but the empty moorland, the distant roar of the turbulent sea, and the melancholy whistle of wind whipping through sparse grass.

In the tomb, however, I hoped for something more. We soon reached the bottom of the passageway, and I blinked in the dim lamplight, peering anxiously ahead while my eyes adjusted to the subterranean darkness. For a moment I could distinguish nothing more than three stone walls of what looked like a plain little chamber. But then, as I stood watching, it happened.

The chamber exploded with color—vivid color. Bright, startling reds and yellows, emerald greens, and deep azure blues swam into view before me. And as I continued to watch, the room magically began to come alive.

One by one, painted figures seemed to step out from the walls. To my left I saw smiling dancers in elegant garments; they were twirling to some silent, frenzied music, full of the joy of motion. On the right were musicians—a dark-haired man in a knee-length mantle was playing a double flute, and another strummed a lyre. They too swayed to their own hypnotic rhythm.

On the main wall before me appeared a festive banquet. Three couples, dressed in colorful cloaks and tunics, lounged on couches, talking and reveling. They were attended by slaves serving wine. A pair of leopards, for which the tomb was named, confronted each other on the wall above the couples. The scene was so zestfully brilliant, so full of movement, that it seemed animate. And so it was intended by the Etruscans, who had prepared this tomb centuries ago to hold their aristocratic dead.

No wonder, I thought, that the English author D. H. Lawrence, who saw these same tombs some 50 years ago, was compelled to write in his book *Etruscan Places:* "To the Etruscan all was alive; the

Overleaf: Eerily lifelike, alabaster figures possibly carved to house the spirits of the dead gaze serenely from the tops of chests holding the ashes of the cremated. The subterranean tomb, discovered near Volterra, a small town in north-central Italy, contained the remains of an Etruscan family of the second century B.C.

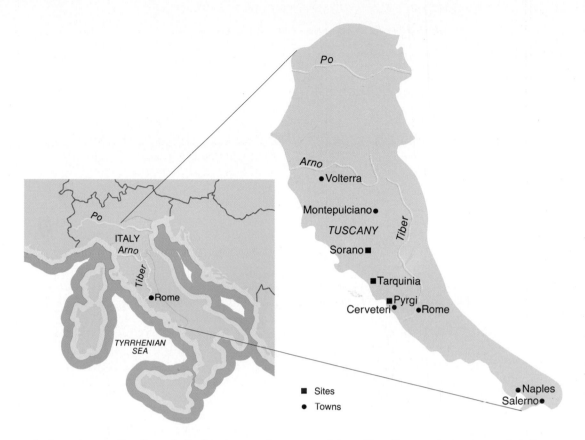

The map shows the locations of Po, Arno, Volterra, Montepulciano, TUSCANY, Sorano, Tiber, Tarquinia, Pyrgi, Cerveteri, Rome, Naples, and Salerno. A sidebar map shows ITALY, Po, Arno, Tiber, Rome, and the TYRRHENIAN SEA.

■ Sites
● Towns

whole universe lived; and the business of man was himself to live amid it all."

"*Bello*—beautiful—*no, signorina?*" asked the young Italian guide, smiling at my astonished face.

I nodded, suddenly remembering his presence and that of my companion, Swedish archeologist Eva Rystedt, who stood quietly beside me.

Eva is preparing a dissertation on Etruscan architectural material. She teaches at the University of Stockholm and has participated in Etruscan excavations directed by the Swedish Institute of Classical Studies in Rome. She had agreed to accompany me on my travels through north-central Italy, the ancient homeland of the Etruscans, where I hoped to find traces of this fascinating people.

The Etruscan civilization, Italy's first, flourished for seven centuries, beginning about 750 B.C. Soon after that date, Etruscan tomb inscriptions began to appear on Italian soil. Earlier, north-central Italy was little more than a tangled wilderness with scattered villages inhabited by Iron Age people called the Villanovans. Then, seemingly all at once, the Etruscans' powerful and sophisticated city-states rose and rapidly spread over the scattered villages of the Villanovan people.

By the sixth century B.C., when the Etruscans reached the peak of their power, they dominated much of the Italian peninsula, ruling territory that stretched north beyond the Po River and south to present-day Salerno.

Conquerors and rulers of (Continued on page 176)

Etruscans, Italy's first civilized people, unified much of the Italian peninsula (yellow area) by the sixth century B.C. Etruscan city-states appeared between the Arno and Tiber rivers beginning about 750 B.C.; but the origin of their civilization remains in dispute. Renowned as merchants and craftsmen, the Etruscans flourished for several centuries—until the Romans, a people they had conquered, grew in power and overwhelmed them.

Sorano, a medieval village built atop the ruins of an Etruscan settlement, perches at the edge of a wooded cliff. To bury their dead, the Etruscans painstakingly carved tombs in the sheer walls of such cliffs; doorways to tombs near Sorano penetrate the soft volcanic rock (right). Etruscans either cremated the corpse or placed it in an underground chamber. In either case, they surrounded the remains with possessions that the deceased had prized and with paintings and sculptures that reflected the vibrancy of Etruscan life.

Under a pavilion beside a dome-shaped tomb, noble Etruscans of about 500 B.C. pay tribute to a deceased relative with an elaborate feast.

Elegant women recline beside their husbands, enjoying wine, fruit, and meat and the entertainment of musicians and dancers. Such behavior apparently shocked early Romans and Greeks, whose wives never participated in feasts or celebrations.

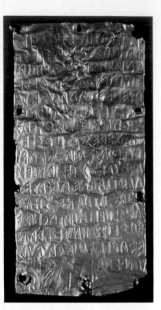

Thin gold tablets—one inscribed in Etruscan (above), the other in Phoenician—record a devotion to a goddess. Linguists hoped that the Phoenician text might provide a key to the Etruscan language. Though the two texts did not correspond word for word and differed grammatically, experts gained clues to word patterns and identified a few terms.

BOTH FROM VILLA GIULIA, ROME

early Rome, then a small frontier town of Latin-speaking people, the Etruscans were great warriors and experienced seamen. Their name appears frequently in the writings of ancient Greeks, who feared their pirate ships. The Greeks called the Etruscans the "Tyrrhenoi," and today that name lives on in the waters that wash Italy's west coast, the Tyrrhenian Sea.

The Etruscans were also gifted craftsmen, who excelled in finely wrought bronze and lifelike terra-cotta and stone sculptures. But above all, the Etruscans were renowned as wealthy merchants. They traded iron, copper, and lead—and products made of these materials—for the luxury items of gold, silver, ivory, and pottery that they loved. These things were brought in trading ships from Syria, Cyprus, Greece, and many cities of the eastern Mediterranean.

Yet who the Etruscans were—immigrants from another land or a native Italian people—has been debated for many centuries. For their luxury-loving culture was strangely different from that of either the sterner Greeks or the early Romans, and so set them apart from their neighboring cultures in the ancient world.

And what the Etruscans themselves may have written of their own early history and of the events that led to the decline of their glittering civilization is largely veiled in mystery. Their language is so different from other tongues that it is still little understood. The Etruscan writings that do exist are mostly short epitaphs and repetitive religious dedications and rituals.

It was therefore to the Etruscans' tombs, the most enlightening remnants of this people, that I had come with Eva. The tombs are scattered over a ruggedly wild region of Italy that includes modern-day Tuscany, a land that also echoes the name of its ancient inhabitants, for the Romans called the Etruscans the "Tusci."

As Eva previously had explained to me, "The Etruscans built their tombs—unlike their homes—of enduring materials. And so most of what we know about these people has come from their graves, which they filled with art and the precious possessions they collected in life."

The Etruscan tombs have often been called "tombs of gold" because of the treasures of gold and silver jewelry, richly crafted bronze artifacts, ivory ornaments, stately sculptures, and imported Greek vases that the Etruscan mighty had buried with their dead. I had spent hours studying the vast numbers of these objects in the museums of Rome and Florence. And they had given me some idea of Etruscan wealth and sophistication.

But it was only in the painted tombs of Tarquinia that I came face to face with the people themselves. In the frescoes there, I saw their image, felt their vibrancy, learned something of their way of life. Slowly they became real to me.

As I studied the banquet scene, I wondered why such a joyous, festive occasion was portrayed in a chamber of death.

"No one knows for sure," Eva said, shaking her head. "Some archeologists think the banquet scene, a common one in these tombs, was painted to represent the actual funeral banquet, which the Etruscans celebrated in honor of the dead. It was obviously an important ceremony, and they probably thought the painting would make this great moment endure forever.

"Others believe that the banquet was painted in the tombs simply to surround the dead person with the pleasurable things he enjoyed in life—friends, good food and wine, and such entertainments as music, dancing, and athletic games. We know from ancient Greek and Roman writers that Etruscan nobles enjoyed such banquets as everyday affairs."

The Etruscans of the great city-states, Eva explained, had a highly stratified society. It was centered on a few wealthy families that owned large amounts of land. These families had great numbers of serfs and slaves who cultivated grain, grapes for wine, olives, and fruit, and raised pigs, cattle, and sheep. From the abundant forests of Italy and from the nearby sea came meat—deer, boar, ducks, and fish. Everything contributed to the gracious living and the sumptuous feasts that the Etruscans relished.

"Greek and Roman writers apparently disapproved of the Etruscans' life-style," Eva added. "To them it was so different, so strange, that it seemed soft and decadent. They especially disapproved of Etruscan women. Look at the women in this painting taking part in the banquet, for example. They were allowed to join their husbands at the banquet, lying beside them on couches, drinking wine, and even proposing toasts."

Such behavior must have terribly offended the Greeks and Romans of the time. The place of their women was definitely in the home, looking after children or spinning wool. Etruscan women were looked upon as improper and even immoral by peoples of these other cultures.

That afternoon, as I walked across the verdant land near Tarquinia and gazed out to the sparkling sea, I kept thinking about the Etruscans. I tried to picture their busy seaports, their elaborate feasts, their lively and appealing women. But most of all, I reviewed some of their puzzling customs. For unknown reasons, the Etruscans did not use lasting materials in building their homes and temples. Yet they painstakingly carved elaborate tombs of enduring stone—tombs that would remain hidden in the earth like time capsules, holding the traces of their lives.

Why? I asked myself that question repeatedly, but I could find no answer.

The question continued to haunt me as Eva and I drove south near the coast of the Tyrrhenian Sea to visit the tombs of Caere, another ancient Etruscan city. We wound among dramatic cliffsides and medieval hilltop towns interspersed with valleys greened by spreading vineyards. As we approached Caere, today the modern town of Cerveteri, Eva told me that we would be seeing one of the largest Etruscan cemeteries, the Banditaccia necropolis, a "city of the dead."

We soon entered a wide plain at the foot of the blue-green Tolfa Hills. In the distance I could see dozens of round humps rising from the ground like giant mushrooms.

"Those are the tombs," Eva said.

As we entered the cemetery, she explained that the Etruscans had piled great mounds of earth on raised stone foundations above burial chambers which had been hewn from bedrock. The earth domes, some as large as a hundred feet across, truly formed a city of the dead. They were constructed along a grid of wide boulevards that opened on small plazas.

The cemetery was deserted and completely quiet. Cypress trees growing among the tombs reached into the sky, their green leaves murmuring in a soft breeze. Wild flowers—bright red poppies, blue-bells, pink orchids—sprouted everywhere, decorating the tombs with life.

I entered one of the largest tombs and found to my surprise that it was dry and warm, not at all gloomy or damp as I had expected. It was spacious, with a high, curved roof. There were several rooms, complete with chairs, beds, and even beamed ceilings carved from solid rock, to represent the interior of an Etruscan dwelling. On the beds, the Etruscans placed the bodies of the dead. Nearby, they arranged the richest possessions of the deceased. Though different from the tombs of Tarquinia, this grave had the same elegance, the same aura of permanence.

As I stood in this impressive tomb, the question of "Why?" again tugged at my thoughts.

Afew days later in Rome I posed my question to Dr. Mario Moretti, a distinguished archeologist who recently retired after 40 years as Superintendent of Antiquities of the Province of Southern Etruria. "Certainly," he began, "the Etruscans believed that the afterlife was much more lasting than the brief span on earth. They therefore would want to make their tombs as eternal as possible. They even used architects to construct them like actual houses.

"To make the afterlife enjoyable, the Etruscans surrounded themselves with the things they loved. The funeral banquet, likewise, was a happy occasion that saluted the dead person in a manner similar to the way he would be honored if alive. There were music and feasting, dancing and games, all in a pavilion right at the tomb site. Everything was intended to comfort and refresh the deceased."

The sophisticated architecture of the tombs, combined with their lavish treasures, led some archeologists to theorize that the Etruscans had immigrated from another land, possibly Asia Minor, and had imposed their culture on the native people. In contrast, Dr. Moretti and most other experts believe that the Etruscans were indigenous people who were strongly influenced by foreign contacts.

"I contend that the Etruscan civilization was born here in Italy, that it grew naturally from the Villanovan culture," he said emphatically. "There were undoubtedly early settlers and traders from the east who brought other customs and ideas to the Villanovans. These were adapted by them and later transformed during the development of the Etruscan culture. But these early immigrants came in small scattered groups, and certainly not in one large mass of people called the Etruscans."

One of the most important influences on Etruscan culture was that of the Greeks, explained Dr. Mario Torelli, a quick-spoken and energetic archeologist who is one of the most respected of all Etruscan experts. "We now have archeological evidence," he told me as we sipped espresso coffee in a cafe in Rome, "that Greek settlers were present on the island of Ischia, off the Italian coast near Naples, as early as 775 B.C. These Greeks came to Italy to trade for minerals, which they lacked. The Greeks were always interested in Italy," he added. "It was a sort of El Dorado to them."

The early Greek settlers brought with them a diversity of products, methods, and ideas. According to Dr. Torelli, these helped account for the rapid rise of Etruscan culture. Among other things, they introduced advanced construction and agricultural technologies—particularly in the cultivation of grapes for wine—brought the pottery wheel, and donated their alphabet.

"In my opinion, the Greek presence was a determining influence on the development of the Etruscans," Dr. Torelli told me.

From the Greeks, the early Etruscans gained an appreciation for valuable objects. Greek craftsmen established workshops in Italy where native artisans learned how to create works of gold, silver, ivory, and bronze.

Although scholars have reached agreement on the derivation of many parts of the Etruscan culture, the language still presents several baffling problems. For the Etruscans spoke and wrote a language that is not parallel to any of the broad groups of languages now identified in the world. Paradoxically, the *letters* of Etruscan writings can be easily recognized, since the Etruscans borrowed and adapted the Greek alphabet. But most of the words, the grammar, and the construction are completely different from those of any other known language. And so the meaning of Etruscan writings, except for funerary inscriptions, remains elusive.

Undoubtedly the foremost authority on Etruscan language today is Dr. Massimo Pallottino, professor of Etruscan and Italian studies at the University of Rome. In his book, *The Etruscans*, Dr. Pallottino writes, "It becomes obvious . . . that we cannot answer the question whether Etruscan has been interpreted or not by a simple yes or no. Our answer will have to be a partial one, shifting and forward-looking: that we know today a good many things about the language but that many others are obscure, that areas of darkness gradually become more circumscribed or clarified as the result of much hard work." Dr. Pallottino adds, "A once-for-all answer would be possible only if we possessed a general 'key,' . . . a known language so close to Etruscan as to explain its roots and forms automatically. . . . In the case of Etruscan, however, there are no documents written in closely related languages."

In 1964 the discovery of the Pyrgi gold tablets, with religious inscriptions written in Etruscan and Phoenician, promised hope as a bilingual key to Etruscan, since Phoenician is an understood language. Although the Pyrgi tablets helped scholars learn grammatical patterns and the meanings of several Etruscan words, the two texts did not correspond word for word.

According to Dr. Pallottino, much of the problem arises because of the brief and complex nature of the existing writings. Even so, "the fundamental basis of research remains the direct examination" of the Etruscan texts themselves to analyze and to reconstruct the rules of the language. Although this is a lengthy and laborious process, he points out that it yields "modest but fruitful advances" each year. Today, several hundred Etruscan words are known. And the promise of further knowledge grows as more inscriptions are discovered.

Beyond the problem of their language, the eventual fate of the Etruscans also has preoccupied scholars. What caused the decline and disappearance after several centuries of prosperity? Conquest? Civil war? Social upheaval?

"They did not just disappear," Dr. Torelli told me firmly. "They were absorbed by the Romans. For Rome eventually overthrew its Etruscan rulers and went on to conquer their cities, as it did in a great many other areas. This is why the Etruscan language, like the languages of several other conquered peoples, simply went out of use. Latin became the cultivated language of all countries in the western Mediterranean.

"Yet the Etruscans themselves did not promptly die out as a people. Many noble Etruscans even became members of the Roman senate, as we know from Latin inscriptions.

"And you must always remember," Dr. Torelli added, "that Rome was once an Etruscan town. Many of the things that became part of the Roman civilization came from the Etruscans."

First among these things, I discovered, was writing, a skill which the Romans learned from their Etruscan teachers, although they did not adopt the Etruscan language. Many Latin words, nevertheless, are derived directly from Etruscan. Among these is *persona*, the Latin word meaning mask. It comes from the Etruscan *phersu*, which may live on in the English word person. The Latin word *litterae*, meaning letters, also derives from an Etruscan word. *Triumphus*, likewise, came to the Romans through the Etruscans, and is the source of the English word triumph.

The cry of "Triumphus" was used to herald victorious Roman generals. Later, it became the name of the Roman procession following military victory, a ceremony originated by Etruscan soldiers. Indeed, the Roman system of organizing armies was developed while Etruscan kings governed Rome. Ironically, the Romans used it to conquer their Etruscan rulers.

The Etruscans also bequeathed to Rome their art, the first sculptures of Roman gods, and their skill in building and engineering. The original Forum, seat of Rome's government, was built by the Etruscans, as were many bridges, roads, and drainage systems. The Cloaca Maxima, Rome's elaborate sewer system that is still in service today, was designed and constructed by Etruscans.

Beyond these legacies, the Etruscans left many rituals, particularly soothsaying—the reading of omens in such things as animal livers, lightning, and the flight of birds.

The Etruscans also passed on to Rome their dress and their symbols of authority. The toga, emblem of Roman citizenship, came from the Etruscan *tebenna*, a shorter version of the loose-fitting cloak. The purple robes and royal scepters of Etruscan kings were adopted by

Roman emperors. And the clothing and insignia of Etruscan priests—the crosier, a staff resembling a shepherd's crook, and the cope, a long ecclesiastical mantle—were adapted by pagan Roman priests. The crosier and cope are still used in the ceremonies of the Roman Catholic Church.

Etruscan heritage, then, in many ways, was at the crux of Roman culture, and therefore of all Western cultures that followed. "Without the Etruscans and their considerable influence on Rome," Dr. Torelli concluded, "our own civilizations, yours and mine, would be vastly different."

Despite the impact of the Etruscans, the myth that they completely vanished persists among some Italians today. For example, I met a youth in Rome who, after questioning me on the nature of my visit and learning that I was studying the Etruscans, said, "Ah, yes. The Etruscans. Nobody knows where they came from. And they just disappeared, didn't they?" Then he shrugged his shoulders and laughed, as if the ancient question were settled.

But another experience a few days later in Volterra, a small hill-top city of Etruscan origin in the heart of Tuscany, indicated, to me at least, that the young Italian was wrong.

I had gone to Volterra with Eva to visit the city's Etruscan museum, the Museo Guarnacci, famed for its funeral urns of stone and terra-cotta. These, I had been told, were decorated with the most realistic sculptures of Etruscan people ever discovered.

Before visiting the museum, Eva and I (Continued on page 188)

Afternoon sun brightens the facade of the Palazzo Bucelli, a palace in the town of Montepulciano. To decorate the palace's lower walls, builders in the 13th century plundered nearby Etruscan tombs for slabs of rock bearing Etruscan inscriptions and for ash urns intricately carved with rosettes, fanciful animals, and other funeral motifs.

Melancholy expressions mark the faces of an elderly Etruscan couple. Molded of terra-cotta in the first century B.C., the 16-inch-high sculpture once rested atop a cremation chest in Volterra. During earlier centuries of Etruscan prosperity, such sculptures showed smiling, confident couples—content in the expectation that death would perpetuate life's pleasures. But as the fortunes of

the Etruscans began to
decline after the fourth
century B.C., the funeral
sculptures became harshly
graphic, the faces anxious.

oyous scenes of life decorate the walls of the painted tombs of Tarquinia, underground sepulchers built for aristocrats. In one chamber of the Tomb of Hunting and Fishing (right), a vivid seascape portrays robust fishermen, leaping dolphins, and wild ducks in flight—a scene that a person from the city of Tarquinia, just five miles from the Tyrrhenian Sea, would have known and loved. Above the seascape, a wealthy married couple attends a family feast; over the lintel of the doorway, genteel sportsmen return from the hunt. In the Tomb of the Leopards

ARCHIVIO INSTITUTO GEOGRAFICO DE AGOSTINI/BEVILACQUA, MILAN (RIGHT); DAN MCCOY, BLACK STAR

(above), three couples attended by slaves recline on couches and savor the delights of a sumptuous banquet. Although their language remains mostly obscure, such painted records reveal the Etruscans' luxurious and exuberant life-style—destined to vanish forever under the stern rule of the Romans.

Stunningly realistic, a bronze bust captures the gentle humanity of an Etruscan noble of the third century B.C. "Skilled and loving craftsmen," the Greek playwright Pherecrates wrote of Etruscan artisans. A winged soothsayer incised on a bronze mirror (above) reads omens from an animal's liver. Foretelling the future became an important part of early Etruscan religion. A terra-cotta figure (left) may represent an Etruscan deity. Discovered in fragments near Siena in the late 1960's, the five-foot-high figure—called the "Cowboy" for its unusual hat—decorated the rooftop of a religious sanctuary in the sixth century B.C.

SIENA MUSEUM (LEFT); VATICAN MUSEUM (ABOVE); MUSEI CAPITOLINI

Sprawling city of the dead blankets hundreds of acres with grass-covered rock tombs—the oldest, from about 700 B.C., topped with mounds of earth. Carved chambers within the tombs resemble the interiors of Etruscan dwellings. Above, visitors follow an ancient path through the cemetery, located near Cerveteri, 20 miles northwest of Rome. Some 2,500 years ago wealthy Etruscans brought their dead here in horse-drawn funeral carriages. These rich and complex tombs, constructed near much simpler graves of the Iron Age Villanovan people, first appeared at the beginnings of Etruscan history. This led some experts to theorize that the Etruscans had migrated to Italy, perhaps from Asia Minor. Most scholars now believe that Etruscan culture evolved from the Villanovan.

had found lodging with an elderly couple, Eugenio and Anna Fontanelli. Their small house sits atop a cliff on the edge of the city, and overlooks a dizzying vista of faraway valleys and hills.

As I talked with Anna, I studied the strong Tuscan features of her face. Like her land, I thought, she was ruggedly handsome.

Later, Eva and I went to the museum, and we quickly located the funeral urns with their lifelike images of Etruscan people. The sculptures showed men and women of every age and physical type—young, old, handsome, ugly. Some of the faces were sad, some serene, some haughty. One urn in particular caught my attention. It portrayed an elderly couple of the second century B.C., two very human and individual Etruscans.

As we gazed at the terra-cotta images of the husband and wife, Eva suddenly exclaimed, "Look at the woman's face! She seems just like Anna. See, the same high cheekbones, prominent nose, and strong forehead."

When I looked more closely, I was startled by the remarkable

likeness. For this 2,100-year-old sculpture truly appeared to be of Anna Fontanelli.

"People say the Etruscans disappeared," I said. "But when you see faces like that, you think, 'No, they are still with us, even now.' "

Never will I forget my experience of that day, and how real it made the Etruscans seem to me—despite the perplexities that still surround them.

Who the Etruscans were and what events in the distant past helped form their brilliant civilization are questions that will prob ably never be completely answered. Yet, in my travels, I had learned much about the intriguing lives of these people and of their importance to my own heritage. I had seen the promise of greater knowledge about them in the future as more of their monuments are studied and more of their language is slowly understood.

And I had discovered that the Etruscans have not left us entirely, that their legacy and maybe even their descendants endure in the land that bears their name.

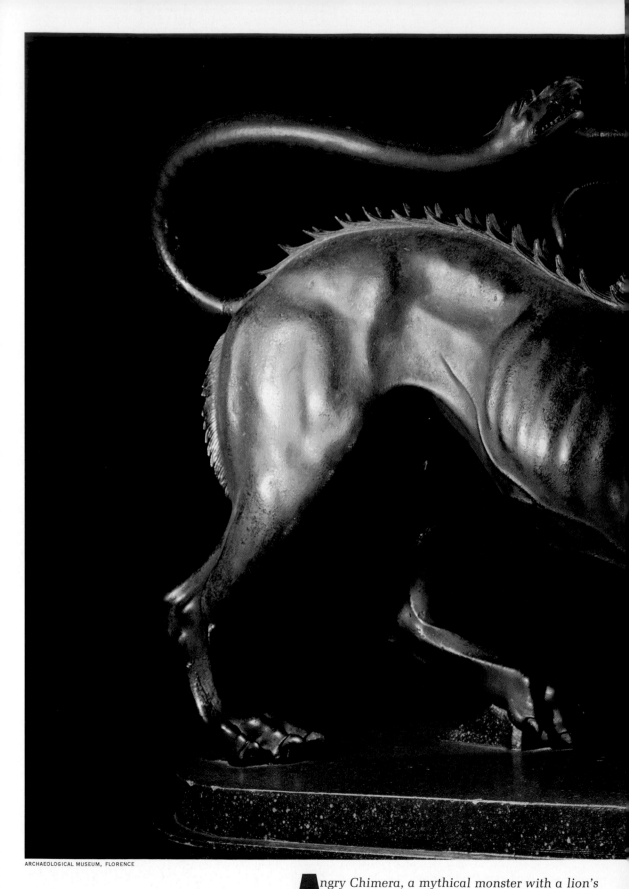

 ngry Chimera, a mythical monster with a lion's body, a serpent for a tail, and a goat's head thrusting from the spine, snarls savagely. The

discovery of this 30-inch-high bronze statue, created in the fifth century B.C. and unearthed in north-central Italy more than 20 centuries later, helped awaken interest in the Etruscans. Lustrous and ornate, the statue reflects the beauty and elusiveness of the Etruscan world.

EASTER ISLAND: BROODING SENTINELS OF STONE

by RON FISHER

photographed by JAMES P. BLAIR

I laughed when I saw the horse, its back swayed but its head held high. Astride it were four people—a matronly woman smiling broadly and three toddlers with grins identical to hers. Their eyes never left me, though the horse was plodding slowly across a grassy plaza fronting one of the wonders of the world.

To them, an American with a camera was more interesting than the great stone statue beneath whose somber countenance they rode. Although the statues of Easter Island may be a mysterious curiosity to the rest of the world, to the Easter Islanders they are a familiar feature of the landscape. Just as I have become accustomed to the monuments of Washington, D. C., so the Easter Islanders of today seem oblivious to their remarkable sculptures.

Easter Island, I discovered, is a gentle land, a special place, and there is something magical in the air. The very name conjures an image of brooding, enigmatic statues. I found myself peering deep into the islanders' eyes, seeking there a hint of their curious past.

For there was a time, only a few centuries ago, when Easter Island was the home of a proud culture, its people engaged in a surge of religious artwork, its society orderly and benign, its small world self-contained and self-sufficient. But within just two centuries a stunning disintegration plunged the society into shambles. Its art was willfully destroyed, civil wars raged, cannibalism prevailed. Its crops were neglected, and the terrified people lived huddled in dark caves, seldom venturing out into the warm Pacific light. From a population of perhaps 10,000, a mere handful survived. After creating the most remarkable complex of religious statuary in the Pacific, the people of Easter Island nearly destroyed their world.

The mysteries of Easter Island, and there are many of them, refuse to yield entirely to the investigations of archeologists, ethnologists, linguists, engineers, and other experts. These enigmas are a litany of who, what, where, how, and—above all—why.

Why were the statues on Easter Island erected, and why pulled down? Who carved them, and where did the people come from? Were they Polynesians, South American Indians, or both? How could a small group of workmen move monuments weighing 20 tons or more across miles of rugged, boulder-strewn country to their sites on the seacoast? And how stand them up? And why cap some with stone topknots? Why do statues stand with their backs to the sea, as if the ocean were too disheartening an expanse to contemplate?

How did the first settlers manage to find Easter Island at all? It is one of the most remote spots on the planet, a 69-square-mile dot lying 2,300 miles west of Chile and 1,300 miles east of Pitcairn Island. According to Dr. William Mulloy, an archeologist who studied Easter Island for many years before his death in 1978, "This is the most isolated island in the world. Anybody who got here, in prehistoric times, was lost—and had to stay."

Delve deeper into the Easter Island society, and you find more puzzles. What is the meaning of the islanders' system of writing—called *kohau rongorongo*—in which rows of hieroglyphic signs were incised on wooden tablets? Why did the islanders, after six centuries of carving statues, turn to a new religion called the Bird Cult? And how can we account for the start of the bloody civil wars that for five

Overleaf: Explosive light of the morning sun bathes Easter Island, home of a culture that rose to greatness and then died in the empty reaches of the Pacific Ocean. This small island lies farther from inhabited land than any other spot on the globe—yet canoe-borne Polynesians somehow discovered and settled it more than 1,500 years ago. According to legends, a chief named Hotu Matu'a led his people here from the central Pacific, navigating always toward the rising sun.

decades pitted tribe against tribe, reducing the populace to terror and killing hundreds?

In 1770 a Spanish navigator named Agüera landed on the island, observed the statues and their topknots, and commented in his journal, "Much remains to be worked out on this subject." The same is true today. The mysteries of Easter Island have been sorted and sifted, argued and debated, but many have yet to be solved.

Easter Island first came to the attention of the outside world on Easter Sunday, 1722, when the Dutch explorer Jacob Roggeveen sighted its jagged coast. He found an island, roughly triangular, with three volcanoes forming its corners. Islanders swam out to his ships and promptly stole the caps off his crew's heads. Many of the company went ashore briefly, scouted around, and then departed. Roggeveen mentioned in his log that the "remarkably tall stone figures . . . caused us to be filled with wonder." Most were fitted with topknots, red stone hats that weigh several tons. He also noted that the people, both women and men, were covered—head to toe, front and back—with paint and elaborate tattoos.

In 1774 Captain James Cook anchored offshore for four days; one crew member observed that some of the people had pierced their earlobes and inserted coiled leaves to extend them, often down to the shoulders. Another reported that the islanders were "expert thieves. . . . It was with some difficulty (Continued on page 200)

Volcanoes anchor the three corners of Easter Island, a mid-ocean speck just 15 miles at its widest. Traditions say Hotu Matu'a and his people landed at Anakena; they gradually populated the island and created a complex society. Towering stone statues honored ancestors, and caves provided burial sites or shelter during times of warfare. Today Chile governs the island, home to some 2,500 people.

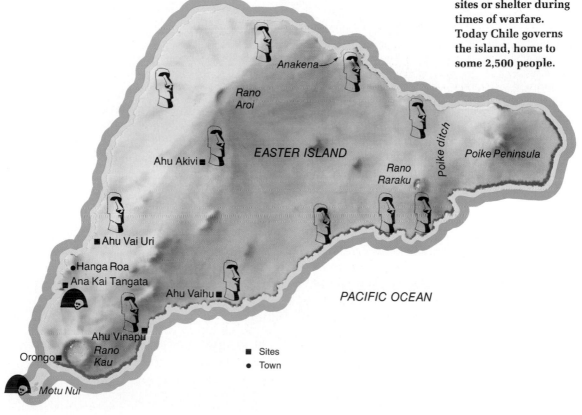

Somber sentinels, massive statues called moai guard the flank of Rano Raraku, the volcanic mountain where islanders carved them. Many

unfinished giants lie imprisoned in stone, abandoned when the work suddenly and mysteriously stopped. Others stand buried to their shoulders in quarry debris and eroding soil and rock. From Rano Raraku, the Easter Islanders moved the moai across rocky terrain to sites along the coast.

Capped by a stone topknot, a 26-ton, 22-foot-tall statue stands regally on its elevated platform. Archeologists reset the moai in 1968. Centuries ago, the islanders built some 250 ahu, religious centers consisting of platforms, ramps, and plazas that they used for important ceremonies. Later, they began erecting statues at these ahu to honor respected ancestors.

Delicately tinted, a double rainbow arches above the rugged stone figures of Ahu Akivi. The moai face a plaza fronted with stones, the site of early religious rites and dances. Once the moai gazed upon grisly rituals, as islanders killed and consumed human sacrifices in cannibal feasts. When civil wars broke out, statues fell along with human casualties: Raiding warriors from different tribes toppled one another's moai, often shattering them in the process. At left, several figures lie where they fell on the coast at Ahu Vaihu. Father Sebastian Englert, a German priest who lived on the island for nearly 35 years, studied the island's history, recorded its artifacts, and painted identifying numbers on many of the statues.

Abandoned in their stone cradles, statues (right) wait through eternity for a stonecutter's finishing touch. More than 200 moai in various stages of carving lie on the slopes of Rano Raraku. Below, a ten-foot figure gazes skyward from the rim of the volcano's crater. *Totora* reeds flourish in the crater's lake, once a source of water for the people. Each of the statues represented a specific ancestor, and had a name. The early islanders called them *aringa ora*—"living faces." Archeologist William Mulloy, instrumental in re-erecting many statues, first came to Easter Island in 1955. After his death in 1978, associates buried his ashes on his beloved island.

we could keep the Hatts on our heads." A French explorer named La Pérouse landed for a day in 1786. "I know not what are their ideas among themselves of the sacredness of property," wrote his surgeon, "but their conduct towards us evinces the little regard which they have for that of strangers; they took such a liking to our hats, that in a very few hours they robbed us of them, and then laughed at us like mischievous school-boys." La Pérouse and his men left behind some pigs, goats, and sheep when they sailed, but the islanders evidently devoured them, for none remained when the next Europeans called.

Many of the explorers reported that the early islanders lived in unique boat-shaped houses. George Forster, a naturalist traveling with Captain Cook, described them: "The foundation consisted of stones about a foot long, laid level with the surface in two curve lines, converging at the extremities. These lines were about six feet asunder in the middle, but not above one foot at the ends. In every stone of this foundation we observed one or two holes, in each of which a stake was inserted."

The stakes were bent, and reeds, leaves, and grasses were woven among them to form a roof. The completed house had much the look of an upside-down canoe. The stone foundations can still be found all over the island, nestled intimately into the grass. A few were as long as 300 feet, and tribal members slept in them.

As with peoples throughout Polynesia, contact with outsiders brought Easter Islanders little but trouble. As with the others, the trouble included the eventual destruction of their society. In the case of Easter Island, the loss is especially frustrating, for many of the answers to the mysteries of the island died with the elders.

In raids between 1859 and 1862, Peruvian slavers hauled off about a thousand islanders—a third of the surviving population—to work in guano mines on islands off the coast of Peru. The Bishop of Tahiti protested, and the islanders eventually were ordered returned to their home. But of the thousand, most had died of disease, malnutrition, and overwork. Only a few reached home, and they carried with them the source of the final catastrophe: smallpox. The disease swept across the island, killing all but a hundred or so people by 1877. Much of what we know of Easter Island's ancient culture was passed down by the descendants of these survivors.

But long before the smallpox epidemic, something else had happened on Easter Island. By the time of Captain Cook's visit, most of the enormous statues had been toppled onto their faces. "Many of them had been tipped over into holes that had been specially dug for them," Dr. Mulloy told me shortly before his death. "It's as though the islanders not only wanted to destroy the statues, but also wanted to get them completely out of sight, to pretend they didn't exist." The vandals decapitated many by tipping them onto sharp boulders placed to strike the monuments' thin necks.

"The early Europeans found a diminished group of people living among the ruins of their former spectacular accomplishments, and paying little attention to them," Dr. Mulloy said.

What on earth had happened here? What could account for a people's deliberately destroying its own culture? For the answers we must look back into the misty legends that survived with the islanders who escaped the smallpox.

According to tradition, a heroic chief named Hotu Matu'a landed on Easter Island after he and his followers had fled their homeland, which lay somewhere far to the west. He had sailed away in an enormous double canoe laden with many people and a supply of chickens and taro roots. Their reason for leaving is unclear. Perhaps there was a natural calamity or internal warfare.

Although the place of their origin is still debated, Easter Island legend says the people came from Hiva. Some 2,100 miles to the northwest of Easter Island are the Marquesas Islands—among them Nuku Hiva, Fatu Hiva, and Hiva Oa.

Other clues also link the Easter Islanders to the Marquesas: The languages are similar, and several types of artifacts—notably fishhooks and adzes—bear a striking similarity. Dr. Yosihiko H. Sinoto, Chairman of the Department of Anthropology at the Bernice P. Bishop Museum in Honolulu, has worked in the Marquesas periodically for many years. In his office in the museum, he told me, "When I first visited Easter Island it was like going home."

But most intriguing of all: In the dank and dripping jungles of the Marquesas, ancient stone statues of roly-poly men gaze endlessly into the gloom. They are very unlike the figures of Easter Island, but perhaps they hint at a statue-carving tradition buried deep within these particular Polynesians.

And it is of course the statues—called *moai*—that have attracted the world's interest to Easter Island. Some 600 of them are strewn across the island. Almost 30 have regained their original grandeur. Archeologists have replaced them atop their stone altars. Many more lie face down in the dirt. Still others are scattered along grassy roads, evidently abandoned while being transported to their intended sites. And still more are found at Rano Raraku, the inactive volcano from which the statues were carved.

The statues were erected on platforms as long as 500 feet. Paved ramps usually abutted the platforms, and grassy plazas—where religious ceremonies were held—spread in front of the statues. There are some 250 of these religious sites, called *ahu*, on the island.

Today, nearly all of the islanders live in the town of Hanga Roa. Indeed, until recently they had to. The bulk of the island was leased to a Chilean sheep-ranching corporation and, instead of trying to fence in the sheep, the managers put a fence around the town and turned the rest of the island over to the animals. Citizens needed a permit to venture outside Hanga Roa. In 1952 the ranch stopped operating, and the island was restored to the people.

The town is a quiet, dusty settlement of some 2,500 people, whose mania for hats, caps, and other headgear seems to have disappeared. Little boys gallop horses bareback up and down the town's dozen or so streets, and a few trucks, jeeps, and motorcycles bounce along behind them. Low stucco houses, painted a variety of pastels, crouch in the thick vegetation along the streets. There are a couple of grocery stores, a post office, a bank, a school, several shops catering to tourists, a restaurant—and two discotheques! Though there is a new and modern hotel, many visitors choose to lodge with one of the local families who take in short-term guests.

I stayed with Rosita Cardinali in her guest house just up the street from the harbor. She pampered me with lobster three times a week and with bananas from a tree in her yard. In the evenings I would wander down to the soccer field and watch ragtag teams have at each other, as waves—unimpeded by thousands of miles of open ocean—exploded against the sunset. Dogs would bark in the growing darkness and sniff at scuttling noises in the brush. One night I heard singing and followed the sound to the school. I sat outside on a stone wall, with the unfamiliar stars of the Southern Hemisphere wheeling overhead, and listened. A group of singers accompanied by guitars and drums was rehearsing melancholy tunes. I heard Hotu Matu'a's name repeated over and over, with awe and longing.

Most of the islanders speak Spanish, for Easter Island today belongs to Chile. They also speak Rapa Nui, a soothing and melodic Polynesian tongue that is adaptable to the 20th century. I learned, for instance, that on Easter Island the word for jeep is *sipi*, pronounced "sheepy." Early Easter Islanders had no name to distinguish their home from other lands, of which they had no knowledge. Every boulder, bay, hill, and cave had a specific name—but not the island itself. Later, people began calling the island Te Pito o Te Henua, the navel of the world. Today, the islanders refer to it as Rapa Nui or Isla de Pascua, the Spanish name for Easter Island.

In a bouncing, rattling sipi I drove along dusty roads around the island, sometimes alone, occasionally with Easter Islanders who acted as guides. In many ways the landscape resembles English moors: rolling, windswept hills draped with stubby grass and splotched with sliding cloud shadows. Hawks, introduced from South America in the 1920's, have flourished and compete with the native birds. They perch on boulders and in trees, or swoop with sudden wide-eyed rancor in front of you.

Prehistoric ruins of various stone structures can be seen everywhere along the roads; the islanders were accomplished builders of more than ahu. There are elevated tombs and crematoriums, circular enclosures in which mulberry trees were grown, conical towers that marked land boundaries, masonry-lined caves used as residences, and even the remains of stone chicken coops.

From a distance the volcano Rano Raraku looks like a beached whale with one side gnawed away. Generations of Easter Island stone carvers reduced the bulk of the mountain appreciably. From a parking area near its base, trails wind upward, taking visitors on a breathtaking hike among the weathered statues. Some 55 of them perch on the west flank of Rano Raraku. Many are all but finished; they stand buried up to their shoulders in quarry debris at the base of the mountain. A spooky aura hangs over them. Touch one and your hand seems to tingle, as though a faint electrical charge lingers in the cool stone.

At first the carving and erecting of these monuments seem a more grandiose project than people with only stone tools and their own muscle power could have accomplished. So a number of theories have been propounded to account for them. They represent the remnants of a vanished civilization, perhaps even Atlantis; or they were built by extraterrestrial visitors; or the early islanders possessed the secret of antigravity, and simply *willed* the statues to move.

But to stroll through the quarry at Rano Raraku is to see the fallacy of extreme theories. The source of the statues is no mystery. They lie about in every stage of completion, from finished behemoths waiting to be transported to others just begun.

I climbed toward the rim of the volcano with Floyd and Linda Thompson, young American Peace Corps volunteers. Both work with the Chilean park service, helping to make the ruins of the island more accessible and understandable to visitors.

"The mystery," said Floyd, "is not how they carved the figures, but how they got them down the mountain once they were finished." Tiers of partially finished statues rose for 300 feet above us, most lying on their backs, but a few standing upright. There must have been a massive labor force at work here, for it is apparent that dozens of the statues were being carved at one time.

More than 200 sculptures can be found in the quarry. The largest—unfinished—is 69 feet long, and would have stood taller than a six-story building.

"The conviction is unshakable," said Floyd, "that one day the work simply stopped. You have the feeling that the carvers just put down their tools and walked away, never to return."

With basalt hand picks, workmen (above) free a carved moai from its rock bed. Another team uses ropes and restraining posts to ease a statue down the flank of the quarry. After covering its back with tattoo-like designs, they will laboriously transport it to an ahu. There (opposite), workers strain to raise a statue a few inches; others hurry to place rocks and rubble beneath it. Eventually, it will stand upright. A noble with a ceremonial staff oversees the work.

He stooped and picked up a rough stone hand pick, a tool the islanders used to chip and carve the rock into a statue. "There are dozens of these scattered across the mountain where they were dropped," he said. "They're made of andesitic basalt."

It is nearly impossible to visualize how Easter Islanders could move the statues down the steep slope of the mountain without damaging them or the ones being carved.

In fact the inability to move them may have contributed to the society's collapse.

"The largest moai being built," Dr. Mulloy told me, "the 69-footer, would have weighed about 270 tons. The workmen may have recognized the futility of carving a figure they could not possibly move—and simply gave up. The religious building compulsion became a little insane. It came to take up so much of the force of the culture that such important activities as farming and fishing were neglected, and the people didn't have enough to eat. You can carry statue-making only so far."

Another explanation has been offered to account for the abrupt end of the statue-carving. A sculpture proportional to and twice as tall as its neighbor weighs eight times as much. Gradually the artists began trimming weight by making (Continued on page 210)

ribes clash in the bloody battle of Poike ditch—a legend supported in part by factual evidence. Two distinct classes of people, perhaps descendants of

different waves of immigrants, lived on Easter Island. The Long Ears, who stretched their earlobes, enslaved the Short Ears. During a rebellion, the Short Ears surprised the Long Ears at dawn and drove them into a wall of fire. Except for one man, all the Long Ears died.

Diabolic figures evoke rituals and grim myths from Easter Island. Intricately patterned figure (above) probably served as a model for human tattoos. Another tattoo model (upper left) bares reed teeth. Grimacing moai kavakava (lower left) depicts the rotting corpse of an ancestor. Moai paapaa (below) perhaps represents the spirit of a woman. During feasts people hung as many as 20 wooden figures on their bodies and whirled in frenzied dances. Today, Marcial Tuki (opposite) carves for visitors. After decades of neglecting traditional art forms, Easter Islanders have begun to take pride in their heritage; Tuki's nephew attended art school in Santiago and now participates in the island's artistic rebirth.

FIGURES FROM PEABODY MUSEUM, HARVARD UNIVERSITY

the moai slimmer. But this meant that the statues began to lose their resemblance to the men they were meant to honor. In fact, they all began to look very much alike. So the workers eventually lost interest.

On the inside of the crater wall stand more statues, facing a large lake choked with *totora* reeds. At their feet are more hand picks. With the exception of the eyes, the sculptures were completed at the quarry—they were carved and smoothed and some were incised with the decorative markings on their backs that perhaps represented tattoos. Then they were transported to their ahu, and only there were the eyes opened. The figures were erected so that their gaze always fell upon the plazas. The ones on the coast had their backs to the sea.

Sooty terns soar in stylized flight on the wall of Ana Kai Tangata, the Cave of the Cannibals. Chilean archeologist Gonzalo

Figueroa sketches the art. Victors in warfare feasted on the corpses of the defeated here, and even in peacetime warriors craving human flesh killed and ate fellow islanders.

During the early years of archeological study on Easter Island, the islanders were able to answer many of the scholars' questions. They knew how the statues were carved—and why—and could explain many apparent mysteries.

But when asked how the monuments were moved, they answered—to a person—"They walked." This response stymied the scientists. It also gave rise to some of the far-out theories calling for antigravity or extraterrestrial help.

The statues are so heavy they could hardly have been dragged across the countryside: They would simply have plowed into the ground. They might have been rolled along on logs, but Easter Island lacks sufficient forests to provide enough logs. It's even been suggested that the people made slippery roadways of mashed taro—but this is hard to imagine.

William Mulloy has devised perhaps the most satisfactory explanation of how the figures might have been transported once they were down the mountain. Imagine a 20-ton statue resting on a log sled and lying face down with its head pointing in the direction you want to move it. A few feet ahead of it, take a couple of hefty logs and lash them together in a simple bipod—an inverted V. Tilt it backward until its apex is directly over the neck of the statue. Suspend a stout line from the apex of the bipod, and fasten it around the figure's neck. Then have a few men with ropes pull on the bipod. As it swings forward, the head will rise slightly off the ground and lurch a few inches forward. Repeat the process a few thousand times, and you've moved a statue.

I passed several monuments that might have been so transported as I drove to Orongo, an archeological site on the slopes of another inactive volcano, Rano Kao, that stands on the southwest corner of the island. As I followed the winding dirt road that ascends the mountain, horses—which outnumber the human inhabitants of Easter Island about two to one—watched passively, flicking their tails at the large but lazy black flies.

On the seaward edge of the volcano rim there is a row of about 50 partially subterranean stone houses. They are long, low, boat-shaped structures, with small crawlways through which the islanders entered. On one side the crater wall drops away to another reed-filled lake; on the other is a sheer drop of nearly a thousand feet to ocean waves thundering against rocks. Three islets lie offshore.

Here at Orongo, Easter Island's most important religious ritual was held each year: the Festival of the Bird Man, which was practiced as late as the 1860's.

In the Bird Cult, which gradually displaced statue-carving as the island's religious expression, people worshiped a powerful creator-god called *Makemake*. Candidates for the exalted position of Bird Man, who possibly represented the god in human form, volunteered from various leading families

After much celebrating, the volunteers or their trusted representatives swam more than half a mile to the largest and farthest of the offshore islets, Motu Nui. They waited, hidden in caves, sometimes for days, for the return of the sooty terns that nested on the little island during the spring. The first man to find an egg, swim through the shark-infested waters to the mainland with it, carry it up the precipitous cliff, and present it unbroken, won the race. He, or the man he represented, became the Bird Man.

According to island traditions, the Bird Man had his hair, eyebrows, and eyelashes shaved off, and his face painted red and black. He lived alone—*absolutely* alone—in a thatch house for a year, gradually acquiring wisdom and power. At the end of a year, he retired and became a respected elder.

A drive toward the north end of the island took me past Poike ditch, presumably the site of an epic and decisive battle between two classes of people—the so-called Long Ears and Short Ears.

There were evidently at least two waves of immigrants, only one of which lengthened their earlobes. They were apparently the dominant group, as most of the moai have long earlobes.

The Short Ears, so the Easter Island legend goes, were nearly enslaved by the Long Ears. They were ordered to clear the Poike Peninsula of rocks to make it suitable for farming—which is supposedly why the area to this day is nearly rock-free. The Short Ears grumbled and plotted a rebellion; but the Long Ears got wind of it and dug a protective trench across the neck of the peninsula, which they filled with dry wood. They planned, if attacked, to set the trench afire as a barrier against the attackers.

With the help of a spy, a woman, the Short Ears learned of the ploy. Many of them stealthily sneaked behind the encampment of the Long Ears. Others created a diversion. When the Long Ears found themselves under attack, they set fire to the wood in the trench—only to discover that they were surrounded. They were all—men, women, and children—forced into the fiery trench. Only one man was allowed to survive. He later married a Short Ears woman, and today their descendants still live on the island.

It has the sound of another far-fetched legend, perhaps devised to account for a naturally occurring depression or for the absence of rocks on the peninsula. But archeologists digging across the area have found evidence: a layer of soil darkened by fire and heavy with charcoal. According to carbon-dating, the fire occurred around 1680, a date that matches the islanders' oral tradition.

The battle of Poike ditch evidently set off the chain reaction of violence that nearly destroyed Easter Island. The people lived scattered along the coast in extended family groups, each with its own ahu and moai honoring ancestors. The men of different tribes began to raid one another's settlements, toppling the moai and desecrating the ahu. Then actual warfare began, with bands of warriors roaming the island, raiding and killing. When it became unsafe to work the taro fields, the crops died and food became scarce. So, in a final desperate step, the islanders turned to cannibalism. Easter Island is one of the few places in the world where cannibalism apparently had little religious or magical significance. It simply served the quest for food.

The people retreated into the many caves that honeycomb the island, living like moles, venturing out only to kill. They were still living largely thus in the mid-1800's when missionaries began to arrive and exert their pacifying influence.

This curious story brings up once again the question of origin. Who were the Long Ears, and who the Short Ears, and why the enmity? Anthropologist-archeologist Thor Heyerdahl has proposed an answer with which few experts agree, but which none can refute totally. He believes Easter Island was discovered and settled at least twice: once by a pre-Inca people who sailed west from South America and once by the Polynesians. He has used several bits of evidence to support his theory:

—Those totora reeds growing in the craters. Easter Island is the only place in the Pacific where they are found. But they also grow on the shores of Lake Titicaca in the Andes, where pre-Inca natives used them for building boats.

—A curious statue at Rano Raraku. When the figure was unearthed by Heyerdahl's workmen, it was found to be unique on the island; nothing else like it was ever before discovered there. The statue was of a man, kneeling and bearded, much smaller than the moai. Heyerdahl compared it to similar sculptures near Lake Titicaca.

—The ahu at Vinapu. I visited this ahu and was struck, like many before me, by the resemblance of its masonry to Inca ruins. Although some other ahu have carved and fitted stones, Vinapu is the most precise and exact. Even Captain Cook was impressed with ahu: "... the workmanship is not inferior to the best plain piece of Masonary we have in England. They use no sort of Cement, the joints are exceeding close and the Stones are mortised and Tenonted one into a nother in a very artfull manner." Artful, indeed. A knife blade will not penetrate between the carefully laid stones.

So Heyerdahl theorizes that South American Indians landed on Easter Island in two different waves, bringing their reeds, gods, masonry skills, and custom of ear extension with them. Later, Polynesians—the victorious Short Ears—landed, destroyed the original settlers, and overturned their statues, but only after they had adopted the beliefs and customs of their predecessors.

The problem is not so much accounting for Inca-like remains as it is accounting for things that have *not* been found. For instance, no Inca-like pottery or tools have been discovered. If the Indians were here by themselves for hundreds of years, there should be much more physical evidence of them and their culture.

The identity of the two groups of people—called the *hanau eepe* and the *hanau momoko*—is complicated by a curious puzzle that occurs in transcribing Rapa Nui. *Eepe* means heavy-set, but it sounds like the word for earlobe, *epe*. Confusion may have crept in from early attempts at documenting the traditions. It may be that the distinction was really between people of two differing body types—slender (momoko) Polynesians and stocky (eepe) South Americans. The earlobe question may be nothing but a red herring.

Shoulder-length earlobes can be seen on the few moai that have been restored and re-erected on their ahu. William Mulloy supervised most of the restoration. In raising the statues, he used a technique little-changed from what must have been the original method of putting them in place. It was demonstrated for him in 1956 by Pedro Atan, an Easter Islander. With the moai lying on its front, workmen levered its head a few inches off the ground. Small rocks and rubble were tossed beneath it. Then the workers repeated the process at the monument's sides. Back and forth they moved, from side to side, gradually lifting the statue a few inches at a time. Eventually the moai attained a level slightly higher than its ahu. Using the same method—a couple of levers and the island's plentiful rocks—the workmen raised the head higher and higher, until the statue could be slid—with what must have been a heart-stopping crunch—onto its base. Imagine it teetering there, while the workers held their breath!

The red topknot was probably inched up to the head by the same method, though there is a possibility that it was firmly lashed to the figure while it still lay on the ground; then statue and topknot both could have been raised at the same time.

Even today the process has changed little, though a crane has replaced the straining men heaving at levers. Not far from Hanga Roa, I watched for several days as a fallen, headless moai was slowly and carefully replaced on its ahu. As the crane lifted it a few inches, rocks were tossed beneath it. Then it was raised a few more inches. Gradually, it assumed a nearly upright position, then was painstakingly placed on its ahu. Finally erect, the statue, though aged and broken, again regally commanded its domain—as it had centuries before.

According to Easter Island legends, Hotu Matu'a's canoe first landed on the island's largest beach, a small patch of sand called Anakena on the northeastern side of the island.

In Rapa Nui, Anakena means July, and that is probably the month in which Hotu Matu'a landed—for the winds of July favor navigation from the Marquesas to Easter Island. At Anakena, surf hisses and gurgles on the sparkling sand. One large moai had been erected there when I visited, restored by Heyerdahl and his crew in 1956. For several months, Sergio Rapu, a young Easter Islander who studied anthropology at the University of Wyoming under Dr. Mulloy, has been working at Anakena. He has made some startling discoveries.

"It looks as though this was once a major ceremonial site," he told me. "We've found evidence that several generations of ahu were built at Anakena. Over the centuries, they were enlarged and built one atop the other. It may turn out to be the oldest site on the island."

Even more remarkable is a find Sergio made shortly after I left the island. A *New York Times* headline announced in July 1978: "Fragments Said to Be Easter Island Statues' Eyes." According to the story, archeologists believe that the figures once had inlaid eyes, with pupils made from the same red stone as the topknots.

Sergio's excavators had found several fragments of white coral, which, when pieced together, formed a 14-inch-long curved object with a hole in its center. Sergio, fiddling with the fragments and musing over their significance, suddenly cried, "It's an eye!" He hurried to one of the statues nearby and, sure enough, the pieces of coral fit neatly into the eye socket.

"The meaning of *aringa ora* or 'living face,' as the statues were called, and the legend of how they were finished now makes more sense," he wrote me. "The statues were 'completed' once they arrived at the ahu. We knew that this 'completion' included carving of the eye orbits, but now that the eye has been discovered we know that the appearance was more like that of a living person than that of a skull."

If Sergio is right—and so far there's no reason to suppose he isn't—the statues on ahu had eyes. The world is in for a slight shock. Through photographs, we have for years been familiar with the famous stone figures of Easter Island; but now, it seems, we will see them as they were meant to be, truly "living faces." After three centuries of blindness, the moai will once again gaze with dull wonder at their splendid little island.

Makemake—the Creator—glowers from the wall of a burial cave on Motu Nui, one of three islets off the southwest tip of Easter Island. Carlos Pizani of the Chilean park service kneels beneath him. Islanders once believed that this most powerful of gods killed and ate the souls of the dead; priests may have placated him by devouring children before him. Human bones still litter the cave. Pages 216-217: Roiling clouds darken the setting sun beyond the moai of Ahu Vai Uri. With their eternal gazes steady and relentless, they symbolize the many mysteries bequeathed us by ancients the world over, and their fixed stares challenge our understanding.

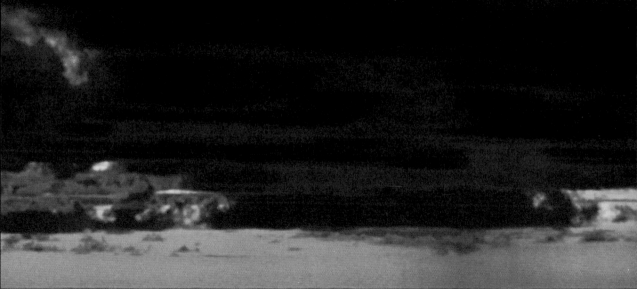

Notes on Contributors

Chicago-born artist ROY ANDERSEN studied at the Chicago Academy of Fine Arts and the Art Center in Los Angeles. His paintings of dinosaurs appeared in the August 1978 NATIONAL GEOGRAPHIC; he also illustrated two recent maps for the magazine—the Southwest and Australia. In 1978 Roy's work was exhibited in a one-man show by the Society of Illustrators in New York.

A graduate of the University of Miami, NATHAN BENN has worked for six years as a contract photographer for the National Geographic Society. Assignments have taken him throughout the United States and to the Middle East three times.

JAMES P. BLAIR in 1978 received the Overseas Press Club award for Best Photographic Reporting From Abroad for his coverage of South Africa, published in the June 1977 NATIONAL GEOGRAPHIC. A staff photographer since 1962, Jim has contributed articles ranging from agriculture in the United States to the peoples of eastern Europe.

CHRISTINE K. ECKSTROM joined the Society's staff in 1974 and has contributed to several recent Special Publications. A native of Philadelphia, she received her bachelor's degree in English from Mount Holyoke College in Massachusetts.

Born and educated in Iowa, RON FISHER has written two Special Publications—The Appalachian Trail and Still Waters, White Waters—and has contributed chapters to Those Inventive Americans, Life in Rural America, and Into the Wilderness.

As often as he can, free-lance photographer ROBERT FRESON leaves his New York studio and returns to his home in Archigny, France. His photographs of the Burgundy region of France appeared in the June 1978 NATIONAL GEOGRAPHIC.

Staff photographer GORDON W. GAHAN joined the Society in 1972; he has traveled on assignment from East Germany to the South Pacific. Gordon photographed A Day in the Woods—a Book for Young Explorers—and contributed to the Special Publication Discovering Man's Past in the Americas.

A free-lance journalist since 1973, LOUIS DE LA HABA previously worked for 11 years as a writer for NATIONAL GEOGRAPHIC. He holds a master's degree in anthropology from George Washington University and contributed a chapter to the Special Publication Clues to America's Past.

TEE LOFTIN, author of the Special Publication The Wild Shores: America's Beginnings, holds degrees in journalism from the University of Missouri and The American University. She also has written chapters for Powers of Nature and The Ocean Realm.

Free-lance photographer FRED MAROON has contributed to periodicals the world over. His own book, The Egypt Story, will be published in April 1979.

TOM MELHAM, who holds a master's degree in journalism from the University of Missouri, grew up on Long Island, New York. Author of the Special Publication John Muir's Wild America, he also has contributed chapters to Powers of Nature and The Ocean Realm.

A member of the Society's staff since 1964, H. ROBERT MORRISON is a graduate of Howard University in Washington, D. C. He was born in Pittsburgh and grew up in central Ohio. Both a writer and an editor, Bob recently contributed a chapter to The Ocean Realm.

CYNTHIA RUSS RAMSAY, a staff member since 1966, has worked on many Special Publications, writing chapters for The Alps, Powers of Nature, and Into the Wilderness. A native of New York City, she received a degree in archeology from Hunter College.

A graduate of the University of Toronto, JUDITH E. RINARD wrote two of the Society's Books for Young Explorers—Wonders of the Desert World and Creatures of the Night. She also has written several Educational Filmstrips and a chapter in the Special Publication Powers of Nature.

GENE S. and GEORGE E. STUART co-authored the Special Publications Discovering Man's Past in the Americas and The Mysterious Maya. Gene, now a staff writer, also wrote Three Little Indians, a Book for Young Explorers. George, the Society's staff archeologist, has done field work in Mexico's Yucatan Peninsula and has contributed articles and maps to NATIONAL GEOGRAPHIC.

Parisian JEAN VERTUT is a nuclear scientist specializing in the remote handling of materials in hostile environments. Since 1949, when he took his first color picture in a cave, he has accumulated some 20,000 photographs of prehistoric cave art and artifacts.

Free-lance photographer ADAM WOOLFITT has contributed articles to NATIONAL GEOGRAPHIC on subjects ranging from Christopher Columbus to New Mexico. A native of England, he now makes his home in London.

INDEX

Boldface indicates illustrations;
Italic refers to picture legends (captions)

Acknowledgments

The Special Publications Division is grateful to the individuals, organizations, and agencies named or quoted in the text and to those cited here for their generous cooperation and assistance during the preparation of this book: Dieter Arnold, William S. Ayres, Emmett L. Bennett, Jr., Larissa Bonfante, Alison S. Brooks, Glyn Daniel, John H. D'Arms, Wafaa el Sadeek, David J. Freddy, Adnan Hadidi, Michel Hamarneh, Peter Harbison, Ronald Hicks, Dorothy Kent Hill, Frances James, Derrick and Susie Johnston, Timothy Kendall, Martin Kilmer, Patrick C. McCoy, Barbara Mertz, Tansu Okandan, Anne Ross, Elsebet Rowlett, Ian A. Todd, Emily Vermeule, Kent R. Weeks, John G. Younger; The Center for Hellenic Studies; French Government Tourist Office, New York; National Museum of Ireland, Dublin; Press Office, British Embassy, Washington, D. C.; Smithsonian Institution.

Additional Reading

ICE AGE HUNTERS: François Bordes, The Old Stone Age; Karl W. Butzer, Environment and Archaeology; J. M. Coles and E. S. Higgs, The Archaeology of Early Man; Jan Jelínek, The Pictorial Encyclopedia of the Evolution of Man; André Leroi-Gourhan, Treasures of Prehistoric Art; Alexander Marshack, The Roots of Civilization; Peter J. Ucko and Andrée Rosenfeld, Palaeolithic Cave Art. JERICHO AND ÇATAL HÜYÜK: Kathleen Kenyon, Archaeology in the Holy Land and Digging Up Jericho; James Mellaart, Çatal Hüyük: A Neolithic Town in Anatolia and The Neolithic of the Near East; Scientific American, Old World Archaeology: Foundations of Civilization. PYRAMIDS: Cyril Aldred, Egypt to the End of the Old Kingdom; I. E. S. Edwards, The Pyramids of Egypt; Ahmed Fakhry, The Pyramids; Sir Alan Gardiner, Egypt of the Pharaohs; Leslie Grinsell, Egyptian Pyramids; Kurt Mendelssohn, The Riddle of the Pyramids; National Geographic Society, Ancient Egypt: Discovering its Splendors. ANCIENT INDIA: Walter A. Fairservis, Jr., The Roots of Ancient India; Gregory L. Possehl, Ancient Cities of the Indus; Sir Mortimer Wheeler, Civilization of the Indus Valley and Beyond and The Indus Civilization. MEGALITHS: R. J. C. Atkinson, Stonehenge; Peter Lancaster Brown, Megaliths, Myths and Men: An Introduction to Astro-Archaeology; Aubrey Burl, The Stone Circles of the British Isles; George Coffey, New Grange and Other Incised Tumuli in Ireland; P. R. Giot, Brittany; Evan Hadingham, Circles and Standing Stones; Gerald S. Hawkins, Stonehenge Decoded; E. C. Krupp, ed., In Search of Ancient Astronomies; Euan MacKie, The Megalith Builders; Claire O'Kelly, Illustrated Guide to Newgrange; Colin Renfrew, Before Civilization—The Radiocarbon Revolution and Prehistoric Europe; John Edwin Wood, Sun, Moon and Standing Stones. MINOANS: Costis Davaras, Guide to Cretan Antiquities; Sir Arthur Evans, The Palace of Minos; Reynold Higgins, The Archaeology of Minoan Crete; Sinclair Hood, The Minoans; J. V. Luce, The End of Atlantis; R. F. Willetts, The Civilizations of Ancient Crete. MYCENAEANS: John Chadwick, The Decipherment of Linear B and The Mycenaean World; Ekdotike Athenon, S.A., History of the Hellenic World: Prehistory and Protohistory; Richmond Lattimore, trans., The Iliad of Homer; George Mylonas, Mycenae and the Mycenaean Age; Heinrich Schliemann, Mycenae and Tiryns; Emily Vermeule, Greece in the Bronze Age. ETRUSCANS: Luisa Banti, The Etruscan Cities and Their Culture; Werner Keller, The Etruscans; Massimo Pallottino, The Etruscans; Emeline Hill Richardson, The Etruscans, Their Art and Civilization; Howard H. Scullard, ed., The Etruscan Cities and Rome. EASTER ISLAND: Father Sebastian Englert, Island at the Center of the World; Thor Heyerdahl, The Art of Easter Island; Thor Heyerdahl and Edwin N. Ferndon, eds., Reports of the Norwegian Archaeological Expeditions to Easter Island and the East Pacific; Alfred Métraux, The Ethnology of Easter Island. Readers may also wish to consult the National Geographic Index for related material.

Library of Congress CIP Data

Mysteries of the Ancient World.
Bibliography p. 220; Includes index.

1. Civilization, Ancient.
2. Antiquities.

I. National Geographic Society, Washington, D. C., Special Publications Division.

CB311.M92   001.9'4   77-93402
ISBN 0-87044-254-6

Composition for *Mysteries of the Ancient World* by National Geographic's Photographic Services, Carl M. Shrader, Chief; Lawrence F. Ludwig, Assistant Chief. Printed and bound by Kingsport Press, Kingsport, Tenn. Color separations by Colorgraphics, Inc., Forestville, Md.; Graphic South, Charlotte, N.C.; National Bickford Graphics, Inc., Providence, R.I.; Progressive Color Corp., Rockville, Md.; The J. Wm. Reed Co., Alexandria, Va.